Mild Korean
순한 한국어

MW00887875

The First Steps to Speak Wild Korean

한글공부방 1급 교재
Textbook for Kongbubang Korean Class Level 1

Written By	Haemin Han
	Sanghyun Ahn
Edited By	Jo-Anna Lynch
Illustrated By	Douglas Holden
Voice Recording By	Moonyoung Heo
	William Lee
	Haemin Han
	Jo-Anna Lynch
	Sanghyun Ahn

ISBN-13: 978-1511814218
ISBN-10: 1511814217

About Mild Korean

Most of the content of this book has been used in the level 1 lessons of the free Korean class, Hangul Kongbubang, for 7 years. Although the content was originally made by Haemin Han, through the years it was scattered and duplicated in different formats, as several teachers used and edited them. Over the past year, the content was rearranged and edited to make a proper language textbook – Mild Korean.

Mild Korean is an entry level textbook and focuses on basic, practical language skills (both written & spoken) required in an average day, wherever Korean is used. There are many, simple conversation exercises for you to practice with friends and classmates. Our goal is to give you fun & easy tools for building the confidence to read, write, and speak Korean, getting you to function in Korean as soon as possible.

한글공부방에 대하여

한글공부방은 한국에 사는 외국인들에게 무료 한국어 교육을 제공하는 봉사 단체이다. 매주 토요일 오후 4시부터 5시 30분 까지, 목요일 오후 7시 30분부터 9시 까지, 서울시 용산구 갈월 종합 사회 복지관에서 수업을 진행하고 있다. 2000년 10월, 외국인을 위한 한국어 교육이 전무한 상태에서 시작한 한글공부방은 2014년 현재 4개 반, 교사 8명, 보조 교사 2명, 1회 평균 학생 수 50명으로 연간 72회의 교육을 실시하고 있다. 한국어 교육과 함께 현장 문화 체험, 역사 교육 등을 실시하여 한국에 대한 이해와 생활 적응력을 높여 '열린 한국'을 실현코자 노력하고 있으며, 한글 공부방 교사 한 사람 한 사람은 민간 외교 사절단으로서의 역할에 자부심을 가지고 활동을 하고 있다.

http://kongbubang.wordpress.com   FaceBook Group – KongBuBang

About Hangul Kongbubang, Free Korean Class

Hangul Kongbubang is a free Korean class for foreigners who are living in Korea. 'Hangul Kongbubang' literally means 'Korean Study Room'. *Bang* means a room in Korean, which is a private place where you feel comfortable. We want to make a relaxed and welcoming place for everyone who wants to learn Korean.

We started our classes in October, 2000 at a small study room, and moved to the present location at Garwol Community Welfare Center in December 2004.

All of our teachers are volunteers. We work or study on weekdays and gather together on Saturdays with the shared passion for helping foreigners learn Korean. We would also like to thank all of our students that join us and encourage us. Learning a language is not that easy, and it's sometimes boring. We want to make your studies a little easier and more interesting.

For more information, please visit the web site http://kongbubang.wordpress.com , or visit the Facebook Group, "Kongbubang".

목차

Table Of Contents

한글 - 모음과 자음

Hangeul - Vowels and Consonants

King Sejong and his scholars invented the Korean alphabet – 한글.

Let's learn about his amazing invention!!!

Also, please note that he is famous for making milk.

Wait, What???

자음   Consonants

	ㄱ	ㄴ	ㄷ	ㄹ	ㅁ
Romanization	g /k	n	d	r/l	m
name of the letter	Gi-yeok	Ni-un	Di-geut	Ri-ul	Mi-um

	ㅂ	ㅅ	ㅇ	ㅈ	ㅊ
Romanization	b	s	ng	j	ch
name of the letter	Bi-up	Shi-ot	I-ung	Ji-ut	Chi-eut

Please note ㅇ has an [ng] sound only when it is used as the final consonant. When it comes before a vowel, it does not have any sound.

	ㅋ	ㅌ	ㅍ	ㅎ
Romanization	k	t	p	h
name of the letter	Ki-yeok	Ti-geut	Pi-eup	Hi-eut

	ㄲ	ㄸ	ㅃ	ㅆ	ㅉ
Romanization	kk	tt	pp / bb	ss	jj
name of the letter	Ssang gi-yeok	Ssang di-geut	Ssang bi-up	Ssang shi-ot	Ssang ji-eut

모음   Vowels

1. Single Vowels

	ㅏ	ㅑ	ㅓ	ㅕ	ㅗ	ㅛ	ㅜ	ㅠ	ㅡ	ㅣ
romanization & name of the letter	a	ya	eo	yeo	o	yo	(w)u	yoo	eu	i

2. Double Vowels #1

	ㅐ	ㅒ	ㅔ	ㅖ	ㅚ
romanization & name of the letter	ae	yae	e	ye	wae (oe)

3. Double Vowels #2

You can guess the sounds of these vowels by pronouncing the two separate vowels together quickly.

	ㅘ	ㅙ	ㅝ	ㅞ	ㅟ	ㅢ
romanization & name of the letter	wa ㅗ + ㅏ	wae ㅗ + ㅐ	wo ㅜ + ㅓ	we ㅜ + ㅔ	wi ㅜ + ㅣ	ui ㅡ + ㅣ

받침　Final Consonants

Final Consonants [pronunciation]	Example Words
ㄱ, ㄲ, ㅋ [k]	박, 밖, 부엌
ㄴ [n]	눈, 산
ㄷ,ㅌ,ㅅ,ㅆ,ㅈ,ㅊ,ㅎ [t]	곧, 끝, 빗, 갔다, 빚, 빛, 좋다
ㄹ [l]	딸기, 물
ㅁ [m]	몸
ㅇ [ng]	방, 강
ㅂ [p]	밥

음절의 구조   Syllable Structure

A Korean syllable is composed of

<u>**CONSONANT + VOWEL**</u> or

<u>**CONSONANT + VOWEL + FINAL CONSONANT**</u>

비	강
ㅂ + ㅣ b i	ㄱ + ㅏ + ㅇ g a ng
consonant + vowel	consonant + vowel + final consonant

안	땅
ㅇ + ㅏ + n no sound a n	ㄸ + ㅏ + ㅇ dd a ng
consonant + vowel + final consonant	consonant + vowel + final consonant

Please note ㅇ has an [ng] sound only when it is used as the final consonant. When it comes before a vowel, it does not have any sound.

연습문제   Exercise

Please listen carefully the audio and practice reading. Please find out what they mean by using a dictionary.

1. Focus on a few basic consonants: ㄱ ㄴ ㄷ ㄹ ㅁ ㅂ ㅅ , with ㅏ.

나라	바나나	사다
나가다	가다	바다

2. Focus on a few basic vowels: ㅏ ㅓ ㅗ ㅜ ㅡ ㅣ.

무	머리	다리
모기	고기	거기

3. Keep Focusing on the same vowels: ㅏ ㅓ ㅗ ㅜ ㅡ ㅣ.

나무	바보	고구마
버스	소리	스시

4. Focus on more vowels: ㅑ ㅕ ㅛ ㅠ and one more consonant ㅇ.

뉴스	교수	벼
여기	요가	우유

5. Focus on more consonants: ㅈ ㅊ ㅋ ㅌ ㅍ ㅎ.

토마토	고추	오리
치마	바지	티셔츠

6. Keep focusing on the same consonants: ㅈ ㅊ ㅋ ㅌ ㅍ ㅎ.

코트	야구	스키
스노우보드	기차	오토바이
스쿠터		

7. Focus on the double vowels: ㅐ ㅒ ㅔ ㅖ ㅚ ㅘ ㅙ ㅝ ㅞ ㅟ ㅢ.

애기	애기	베개
예의	예외	왜

8. Keep focusing on the double vowels: ㅐ ㅒ ㅔ ㅖ ㅚ ㅘ ㅙ ㅝ ㅞ ㅟ ㅢ.

위치	의자	의사
내	개	게
외우다		

9. Focus on final consonants.

부엌	군인	곧
약	산낙지	학교

10. Keep focusing on final consonants.

빗	갔어요	이메일
낮	블로그	집
밥	곱창	

11. Keep focusing on final consonants.

물	운동	김치
조깅	학생	참치

12. Focus on double consonants and confusing sounds.

가래	카레	깨
개	코끼리	꿈

13. Keep focusing on double consonants and confusing sounds.

달	탈	딸
돌	털	덜
통	똥	

14. Keep focusing on double consonants and confusing sounds.

방	빵	곰팡이
아파	아빠	아바

15. Keep focusing on double consonants and confusing sounds.

사요	싸요	
자요	짜요	차요
비	피	벼
뼈		

제 0 과   한국어와 영어의 간단한 비교
Lesson 0   Brief Comparison of Korean and English

Before we go into the lessons, it would be better to take a glimpse at the differences between Korean and English.

1. Verb Comes Last

혜민	피자	먹어요.
Haemin	Pizza	Eats
Subject	Object	Verb

Verbs come at the end of sentences and clauses.

2. Honorifics

To say "I drink beer", you can say one of these.

저 맥주 마십니다.	Polite & formal	저 : I, me (politer than 나)
저 맥주 마셔요.	Polite & less formal	
나 맥주 마셔.	Impolite & informal	나 : I, me

The formal and polite form is rarely used in real life. You can hear this form on the news on TV.

The less formal and polite form is commonly used in daily life. You can use this form to almost anyone in most situations.

The informal and impolite form is used among close friends of similar age. You can also use it to someone younger than you in some situations.

In this book, we will mainly teach the polite, less formal form.

3.　Markers

에이미<u>가</u> 피자를 먹어요.　Amy eats pizza.

　　　　　　가 : subject marker　　　를 : object marker

저<u>는</u> 한국어를 공부해요.　I study Korean.

　　　　　　는 : topic marker　　　를 : object marker

Markers indicate the subject, object and the topic of the sentence.

Many markers are easily omitted in conversational Korean, however, in formal written Korean, they should always be used.

4.　Sentence Order of Question = Sentence Order of Question

Q.　줄리앙 (Julien)　뭐 (what)　먹어요? (eat?)　What does Julian eat?

A.　줄리앙 (Julien)　고기 (meat) 먹어요.(eat)　Julien eats meat.

The sentence structure of questions and statements are the same. You need to raise the tone of the last part of question phrase. You need to lower the tone of the last part in a statement.

제 1 과   저는 혜민이에요.

Lesson 1   I am Haemin.

Making a new friend is one of the best ways to start learning a language. Let's go out and make friends! Before that, we should learn some basic expressions to get to know other people.

중요한 표현   Key Expressions

이름이 뭐예요?   What is your name?

저는 혜민이에요.   I am Haemin.

대화   Dialog

혜민 : 안녕하세요.

　　　만나서 반가워요.

안녕하세요 : hi, hello

만나서 반가워요 : nice to meet you

말리 : 네. 안녕하세요.

　　　이름이 뭐예요?

네. yes

이름 : name　　　~이 : subject marker

뭐예요? : what is ~?　　뭐 : what

혜민 : 저는 혜민이에요.

저 : I (polite form)　　　~는 : topic marker

말리 : 저는 말리예요.

~이에요/예요 : is/am/are~

혜민 : 어느 나라 사람이에요?

어느 : which　　나라 : country　사람 : person

말리 : 미국 사람이에요.

미국 : USA

다양한 표현   More Expressions

안녕히 계세요.   Good bye/ Stay well. (When you are leaving)

안녕히 가세요.   Good bye/ Go well. (When the other person is leaving)

또 봐요.   See you again.

감사합니다 / 고맙습니다.   Thank you.

미안합니다 / 죄송합니다.   I am sorry.

발음   Pronunciation

이름이 [이르미]   사람이에요 [사라미에요]

어휘   Vocabulary

1. 인칭대명사   Personal Pronouns

나	I, me		저	I, me (politer than 나 , humble expression)
너	you			
그	he, him		그녀	she, her
Name 씨	Mr. / Miss / Mrs. Name		ex. 혜민 씨 : Miss Haemin	
이 사람	this person		저 사람	that person
이 분	this person (polite)		저 분	that person (polite)
이 남자	this man		저 남자	that man
이 여자	this woman		저 여자	that woman

그 and 그녀 are rarely used in conversational Korean. Instead of 그 and 그녀, please use ~ 씨, 이 남자, 저 사람, etc.
너 can be used to close friends or someone younger. 너 itself is casual, and you cannot use this to someone elder than you. Instead of 너, it is better to use ~ 씨.

For more information about 이~ and 저~ , please see page 27.

2. 나라 이름   Country

한국	South Korea		나라	country
북한	North Korea		러시아	Russia
일본	Japan		미국	USA
중국	China		캐나다	Canada
대만	Taiwan		호주	Australia
필리핀	The Philippines		뉴질랜드	New Zealand

제 1 과   저는 혜민이에요.

인도네시아	Indonesia	영국	U.K
싱가폴	Singapore	독일	Germany
홍콩	Hong Kong	프랑스	France
인도	India	이태리	Italy
말레이시아	Malaysia	스페인	Spain
베트남	Vietnam	태국	Thailand
콜롬비아	Colombia	멕시코	Mexico
코스타리카	Costa Rica	캄보디아	Cambodia

> By putting 사람 behind of the name of country, you can mean the nationality.
> Ex.   한국사람 : Korean person   중국사람 : Chinese person

3. 언어   **Language**

By putting 어 behind of the name of country, you can mean the language.

한국어	Korean	영어	English
일본어	Japanese	프랑스어	French
러시아어	Russian	중국어	Chinese
태국어	Thai	이태리어	Italian
스페인어	Spanish	독일어	German

> 멕시코 사람이에요? 멕시코어 해요?   Are you a Mexican? Do you speak Mexican?
>
> This question sounds stupid, but it kind of sounds natural to traditional or naive or brainless Korean people, as many countries around Korea have their own languages. Japan-Japanese, China-Chinese, Mongolia-Mongolian, Russia-Russian, Thailand-Thai and Vietnam-Vietnamese. Please do not be disappointed or angry, please just explain the situations in your country.

4. 직업   **Job**

선생님	teacher	학생	student
회사원	office worker	연구원	researcher
군인	military personnel	공무원	government official
가수	singer	배우	actor

문법   Grammar

1.   Present Tense of ~이다 Verb   ~이에요/예요

~ 이다 is like "to be ~" in English. To conjugate ~이다 in the present tense, see the instructions below.

A. Noun ending with a vowel + 예요

저는 말리예요. I am Molly.

나는 조안나예요. I am Jo-Anna.

B. Noun ending with a consonant + 이에요.

저는 혜민이에요. I am Haemin.

나는 아솔이에요. I am Asol.

> Please note you can put only nouns in front of ~이다.

2. Topic Marker   Noun + 은/는

The topic maker indicates the topic of the sentence. In many cases, the topic is the subject of the sentence. Or you can suggest a new topic or change the topic by using this topic marker. Please remember that you can easily omit this topic marker in conversational Korean.

A. Noun ending with vowel + 는

저는 호주사람이에요. I am Australian.

B. Noun ending with consonant + 은

혜민은 한국사람이에요. Haemin is Korean.

3. What is ~   Noun + 이/가 or 은/는 뭐예요?

Use 뭐 like the English word "what" when asking questions. 무엇 is the original form of 뭐. In conversational Korean, it is more natural to use 뭐 instead of 무엇.

Ex. 이름이 뭐예요? What is your name?

직업이 뭐예요? What is your job?

연습문제   Exercise

1. Please use the suggested names and make sentences like the example below.

   Ex. 혜민 > 저는 혜민<u>이에요</u>.

   마이크 > 저는 마이크<u>예요</u>.

   A. 상현

   B. 영숙

   C. 스테파니

   D. 에이미

   E. Use your own name

2. Please see the suggested names, guess their nationality. Connect matching
   nation and make sentences like the example below.

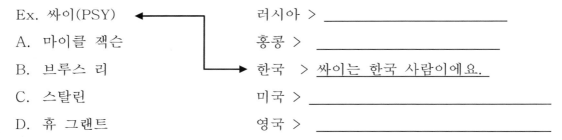

   Ex. 싸이(PSY)   러시아 > _____

   A. 마이클 잭슨   홍콩 > _____

   B. 브루스 리   한국 > <u>싸이는 한국 사람이에요.</u>

   C. 스탈린   미국 > _____

   D. 휴 그랜트   영국 > _____

3. Please exercise conversation with your partner like the example below.

   A : 이름이 뭐예요?

   B : 저는 <u>영숙</u>이에요.

   A : 저는 <u>말리</u>예요.

   B : <u>말리 씨</u>는 어느 나라 사람이에요?

   A : 저는 <u>미국 사람</u>이에요. <u>영숙 씨</u>는 어느 나라 사람이에요?

   B : 저는 <u>한국 사람</u>이에요.

4. Please ask the following questions to each person in the class and fill in the chart.

    A. 이름이 뭐예요?

    B. 어느 나라 사람이에요?

    C. 직업이 뭐예요?

이름 name	국적 nationality	직업 job
말리	미국	선생님
혜민	한국	가수

5. Using the table you just filled in above, please ask and answer other people's name, nationality and job like the example below.

    Ex. 이 사람은 이름이 뭐예요? What is this person's name?

        혜민 이에요. She is Haemin.

        말리 씨는 어느 나라 사람이에요? Where is Molly from?

        말리 씨는 미국 사람이에요. She is American.

        혜민 씨는 직업이 뭐예요? What is Haemin's job?

        혜민 씨는 가수예요. She is a singer.

Movie Review – Please Teach Me English
영화 리뷰 – 영어 완전 정복

By Jo-Anna Lynch

I was recently lucky enough to catch the 2003 Korean film called "Please Teach Me English" (영어완전정복) on TV several days ago. It's definitely a must see for every English teacher working in Korea. It gives a little insight into how Korean adults feel as they attempt to conquer the English language.

It's the story of a Korean man and woman who sign up for an English class at a hagwon. The girl, named "Candy" works in a government office and often needs to deal with foreigners who have problems. The man, named "Elvis", will soon meet his sister who was put up for adoption as a baby and grew up in America. Both want to speak English badly, but both struggle something terrible with the language. Their native speaker teacher isn't much help to them either and quickly gets frustrated with their lack of progress.

Elvis is a bit obsessed with the beautiful English teacher, but Candy has eyes only for Elvis. Unfortunately, Candy is a very awkward, geeky gal with no coordination or tact... her every effort to catch the attention of Elvis goes unrewarded. However, he does discover that while he's totally unattracted to her, he can actually think of her as a friend. The two of them try to learn English and deal with their own personal problems together.

This movie is an oldie but goodie. It's worth tracking down and watching if you can. If you've got some basic Korean skills, you may not even need subtitles since the characters spend most of the movie trying to speak English (however, sometimes being able to read the Korean subtitles is useful to figure out what they are trying to say). Anyone who has taught English in Korea will definitely relate to the characters, particularly one side character who has a problem with his electricity bill.

제 2 과   이게 뭐예요?

Lesson 2   What Is This?

You may want to know the Korean words for many objects. Asking how to say them in Korean using Korean is a good way to learn. Let's act like a three-year old child who is curious everything around him.

중요한 표현   Key Expressions

이게 뭐예요?   What is this?

이 사람이 누구예요?   Who is this person?

대화   Dialog

매튜 : 이게 뭐예요?

이게 : this   contraction of 이것이

이것 : this thing   ~이 : subject marker

이 ~ : this ~

뭐 : what   뭐예요? : what is ~ ?

소영 : 책이에요.

책 : book

~이에요/예요 : is ~   basic form "~이다"

매튜 : 무슨 책이에요?

무슨 : what kind of

소영 : 한국어 책이에요.

한국어 : Korean language

매튜 : 누구 거예요?

누구 : who   ~ 거 : ~'s thing

누구 거 : whose thing

소영 : 앤디 거예요.

앤디 거 : Andy's thing

매튜 : 앤디가 누구예요?

~가 : subject marker

소영 : 저 사람이에요.

저 : that   사람 : person

다양한 표현   More Expressions

이거 영어로 뭐예요?   What is this in English?

이거 한국어로 뭐예요?   What is this in Korean?

모르겠어요.   I don't know. / I don't understand.

몰라요.   I don't know.

알겠어요.   I got it. / I understand.

알아요.   I know

발음   Pronunciation

책이에요 [채기에요]   한국어 [한구거]

누구 거예요? [누구 꺼예요]

어휘   Vocabulary

1. Additional Vocabulary for this lesson

책	book	돈	money
물	water	칠판	white/blackboard
핸드폰	cell phone	지우개	eraser
시계	clock	연필	pencil
안경	glasses	사진	photo
여권	passport	가방	bag
공책	notebook	친구	friend
칫솔	toothbrush	영어	English
치약	toothpaste	한국어	Korean
거울	mirror	의자	chair
책상	desk	달력	calendar
볼펜	ball pen	필통	pencil case

2. 이 / 저 / 그   This / That (visible) / That (visible or not visible)

Like "this" and "that" in English, you can use 이, 그 or 저 depending on where an object is located between the speaker and listener.

이 means "this" for an object close to the speaker.

저 means "that" for an object far away from the speaker.

For 저 and 이, the object should be visible for both the speaker and the listener.

제 2 과   이게 뭐예요?

Use 그 like "that" for something/someone that the listener and speaker both know or obviously see together. It does not need to seen by the listener or the speaker. When speaking, the contraction of 이것이/그것이/저것이 are 이게, 그게, 저게 (this thing, that thing, that thing).

이	this (demonstrative adjective)		
이것 + 이 (subject marker) > 이게 (spoken)		이것	this thing (written)
이것 + 은 (topic marker) > 이건 (spoken)		이거	this thing (spoken)
이 남자	this man	이 여자	this woman
이 사람	this person	이 친구	this friend

저	that (demonstrative adjective)		
저것 + 이(subject marker) > 저게 (spoken)		저것	that thing (written)
저것 + 은(topic marker) > 저건 (spoken)		저거	that thing (spoken)
저 시계	that watch	저 사진	that photo

그	that (demonstrative adjective)		
그것 + 이(subject marker) > 그게 (spoken)		그것	that thing , it (written)
그것 + 은(topic marker) > 그건 (spoken)		그거	that thing , it (spoken)
그 의자	that chair	그 가방	that bag

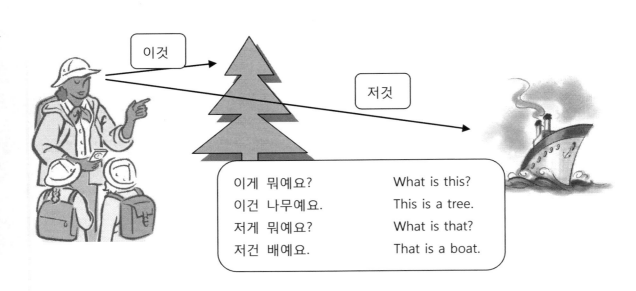

이것

저것

이게 뭐예요?	What is this?
이건 나무예요.	This is a tree.
저게 뭐예요?	What is that?
저건 배예요.	That is a boat.

The topic markers 은, 는; and subject markers 이 and 가, are very confusing for beginners. Always remember that they can be omitted in many cases of spoken language like the example below.

Without Markers	이거 나무예요.	This is a tree.
With topic markers	이건 나무예요.	This is a tree.
With subject markers	이게 나무예요.	This is a tree.

3. 내, 제, 내거, 누구거   Possessive

나	I, me	내	my
내 거	mine	내 핸드폰	my mobile phone

이 핸드폰은 내 거예요. This mobile phone is mine.

저건 내 시계예요. That is my watch.

저	I, me (polite, formal)	제	my (polite, formal)
제 거	mine (polite, formal)	제 친구	my friend

저 가방은 제 거예요. That bag is mine.

이 사람은 제 친구예요. This person is my friend.

이 사람 거	this person's thing	저 사람 거 that person's thing
a person's name + 거	a thing that belongs to a person	

이 여권은 제임스 거예요. This passport is James'.

누구	who, whose, whom	
누구 거	whose thing	누구 여권 whose passport

이 여권은 누구 거예요? To whom does this passport belong to?

이건 누구 여권이에요? Whose passport is this?

문법   Grammar

1. Subject Marker   Noun + 이/가

In Korean, the subject of a sentence is identified by a subject marker 이/가.

If the subject ends in a vowel, use ~가, and when it ends in a consonant, use ~이.

Ex. 마크 씨가 미국사람이에요.   Mark is American.

선생님이 한국사람이에요.   The teacher is Korean.

Subject Marker 이/가   Vs. Topic Marker 은/는

~이/가 is a subject marker, it simply identifies the subject of a sentence. It may emphasize the subject. The focus is usually on the subject.

누가 한국사람이에요?   Who is Korean?

선생님이 한국사람이에요.   The teacher is Korean.

By using 은/는 (topic marker), you can suggest the topic of a sentence. The focus is usually on the explanation about the topic.

선생님이 어느 나라 사람이에요?   Where is the teacher from?

선생님은 한국사람이에요.   As for the teacher, she/he is Korean.

When you contrast two statements, then you need to use 은/는 (topic marker)

저는 한국사람이에요. 마이클은 미국사람이에요. I am Korean. Michael is American.

When you want to change the topic in the middle of conversation, you need to use 은/는.

A: 이게(이것이) 뭐예요?   What is this?

B: 책상이에요.   It is a desk.

A: 저건(저것은) 뭐예요?   What is that?

B: 컵이에요.   It is a cup.

Even if you don't fully understand these grammar points, don't worry. It would be better to let them go for this moment, because these are often dropped in conversation. I hope you learn how to use topic markers and subject markers naturally by noting when native Koreans use them rather than memorizing this grammar point.

---

2.   What Is This/That?   이게/저게 뭐예요?

이것 means this thing. If you put the subject marker for 이것, it becomes 이것이.

In spoken Korean, you can say 이게 for 이것이.

이것 + 이 > 이것이 > 이게 > 이게 뭐예요?   What is this?

저것 + 이 > 저것이 > 저게 > 저게 뭐예요?   What is that?

그것 + 이 > 그것이 > 그게 > 그게 뭐예요?   What is it (that)?

3.   Who / Whose ~   누구 ~

The question word 누구 is both the English equivalent of "who" and "whose."

When asking "who" someone is, use 누구 with 예요. When asking who something

belongs to (whose), place 누구 in front of the possessed noun.

Ex. 저 사람은 누구예요?   Who is that person?

   이게 누구 가방이에요?   Whose bag is this?

4.   What Kind of ~   무슨 + Noun

When asking about the details or characteristics of something, use the question

word 무슨 followed by the noun you want to know more about.

Ex. 저게 무슨 영화예요?   What kind of movie is that?

   호러 영화예요.   It's a horror movie

연습문제　Exercise

1. Please point at an object and ask your partner what it is called in Korean and English like the example below.

   Ex. Q. 저게 뭐예요?　　　　　A. 저건 여권이에요.

   　　Q. 이게 한국어로 뭐예요?　A. 그건(이건) 한국어로 여권이에요.

   　　Q. 이게 영어로 뭐예요?　　A. 그건(이건) 영어로 'passport'예요.

2. Please use the suggested vocabulary and ask your partner about whose things they are like the example below.

시계 watch, clock	여권 passport	핸드폰 cell phone
볼펜 ball pen	노트북 laptop	신발 shoes
지갑 wallet	책 book	맥주 beer
물 water	안경 glasses	컵 cup
숟가락 spoon	젓가락 chopsticks	음식 food

   Ex. Q. 이건 누구 시계예요?　　A. 그건 마이크 거예요.

   　　Q. 저 핸드폰은 누구 거예요?　A. 그건 제 거예요.

   A. Q. 이 지갑은 누구 거예요?　A. ＿＿＿＿＿＿＿＿＿＿＿.

   B. Q. 저건 누구 신발이에요?　A.＿＿＿＿＿＿＿＿＿＿＿.

   C. Q. ＿＿＿＿＿＿＿＿＿?　A. 그건 제 신발이에요.

   D. Q. ＿＿＿＿＿＿＿＿＿?　A.＿＿＿＿＿＿＿＿＿＿＿.

3. Please use the suggested vocabulary and answer the question like the example below.

> 음악 music   가요 k-pop   팝송 pop song   클래식 classical music
> 영화 movie   코메디영화 comic movie   액션영화 action movie
> 책 book   한국어 교재 Korean textbook   소설 novel
> 음식 food   한국음식 Korean food   돼지갈비 Korean style pork bbq

Ex. 이게 무슨 책이에요?

한국어 교재이에요.

A. 이게 무슨 음악이에요?

B. 이게 무슨 영화예요?

C. 이게 무슨 음식이에요?

An Old-Fashioned Junk Food – 뽑기

The guy in the drawing is making 뽑기. It is made by heating up sugar and adding

baking soda. Then it is put on a plate and pressed flat

with a round metal plate. Finally, a special shape is

pressed on it, like this picture on the right.

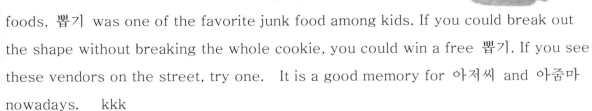

It sounds disgusting but it is quite delicious and addicting.

In the 70's and 80's there were many 뽑기 vendors on

the streets. When there were not many options of junk

foods, 뽑기 was one of the favorite junk food among kids. If you could break out

the shape without breaking the whole cookie, you could win a free 뽑기. If you see

these vendors on the street, try one. It is a good memory for 아저씨 and 아줌마

nowadays.   kkk

제 3 과   남자친구 몇 명 있어요?

Lesson 3   How Many Boyfriends Do You Have?

Numbers are essential to survival in Korea. Please remember there are two kinds of number systems in Korean – Korean numbers and Chinese numbers.

Seriously?? Yes, it is true. Let's learn about the Korean number system first.

How many boy or girlfriends do you have?   The more the better.

중요한 표현   Key Expressions

몇 살이에요?   How old are you?

남자친구 있어요?   Do you have a boyfriend?

남자친구 몇 명 있어요?   How many boyfriends do you have?

대화   Dialog

에이미 : 몇 살이에요?

몇 : what number ~ / how many ~

살 : counting unit for age

줄리앙 : 스물 일곱 살이에요.

스물 일곱 : 27 (Korean number)

~이에요 : is ~

에이미 : 나는 스물 네 살이에요.

스물 네 : 24 (Korean number)

줄리앙 : 남자친구 있어요?

남자친구 : boyfriend   있어요? : have? / is there?

에이미 : 네. 있어요.

줄리앙 : 남자친구 몇 명 있어요?

명 : counting unit for people

에이미 : 세 명 있어요.

세 : 3 (Korean number)   세 명 : 3 people

다양한 표현   More Expressions

시간 있어요?   Do you have time?

남자친구/여자친구 없어요.   I don't have a boyfriend/girlfriend.

많아요.   I have many. / There are many.

몇 분이세요?   How many people are you? (How many people are in your group/party)

발음   Pronunciation

몇 살이에요 [며싸리에요]   일곱 살이에요 [일곱싸리에요]

몇 명 [면명]   있어요 [이써요]   여덟 [여덜]

어휘   Vocabulary

1. 숫자   Number

	Chinese	Korean		Chinese	Korean
1	일	하나 (한)	20	이십	스물 (스무)
2	이	둘 (두)	30	삼십	서른
3	삼	셋 (세)	40	사십	마흔
4	사	넷 (네)	50	오십	쉰
5	오	다섯	60	육십	예순
6	육	여섯	70	칠십	일흔
7	칠	일곱	80	팔십	여든
8	팔	여덟	90	구십	아흔
9	구	아홉	100	백	백
10	십	열	1,000	천	천
20	이십	스물 (스무)	10,000	만	만
21	이십 일	스물 하나 (스물 한)	100,000	십만	십만
28	이십 팔	스물 여덟	1,000,000	백만	백만
33	삼십 삼	서른 셋 (서른 세)	10,000,000	천만	천만
44	사십 사	마흔 넷 (마흔 네)	100,000,000	억	억
153	백 오십 삼		58,000	오만 팔천	
387	삼백 팔십 칠		370,000	삼십 칠만	
3,429	삼천 사백 이십 구		2,571,000	이백 오십 칠만 천	

✓ For all values over 99, Chinese based numbers are used.

✓ In front of counting units, the Korean numbers '하나, 둘, 셋, 넷 and 스물' become '한, 두, 세, 네 and 스무', respectively.

✓ Use Chinese numbers for 분 (minute), 초 (second), 일 (day), 월 (month), 년 (year), 원 (won, money), 인분 (amount of food for the number of people), 층 (floor)

✓ Use Korean numbers for other counting units, under 100

2. Counting Units

	개 thing	명 people	분 people	마리 animal
1	한 개	한 명	한 분	한 마리
2	두 개	두 명	두 분	두 마리
3	세 개	세 명	세 분	세 마리
4	네 개	네 명	네 분	네 마리
5	다섯 개	다섯 명	다섯 분	다섯 마리
20	스무 개	스무 명	스무 분	스무 마리
21	스물한 개	스물한 명	스물한 분	스물한 마리

	잔 glass	권 book	병 bottle	장 paper
5	다섯 잔	다섯 권	다섯 병	다섯 장
7	일곱 잔	일곱 권	일곱 병	일곱 장
8	여덟 잔	여덟 권	여덟 병	여덟 장
12	열두 잔	열두 권	열두 병	열두 장
23	스물세 잔	스물세 권	스물세 병	스물세 장
34	서른네 잔	서른네 권	서른네 병	서른네 장
48	마흔여덟 잔	마흔여덟 권	마흔여덟 병	마흔여덟 장

Ex.

	correct expression	wrong expression
3 cats	고양이 세 마리	세 고양이
5 books	책 다섯 권	다섯 책
1 apple	사과 한 개	한 사과
10 bottles of soju	소주 열 병	열 병 소주 / 열 소주
3 sheets of paper	종이 세 장	세 장 종이 / 세 종이

문법   Grammar

1.   Existence and Possession   Noun + 있어요/없어요

"~ 있어요" means "have ~ " or "~ exists" or "There is ~ ".

"~ 없어요" means "not have ~ " or "~ doesn't exist" or "There is not ~ ".

Basic form of "있어요" is "있다" . "있다" means "to exist / to have".

Basic form of "없어요" is "없다" . "없다" means "to not exist / to not have".

Ex. 맥주 있어요? Do you have beer?

맥주 없어요. 와인 있어요. We don't have beer. We have wine.

여자친구 있어요? Do you have a girlfriend?

여자친구 없어요. 남자친구 있어요. I don't have a girlfriend. I have a boyfriend.

시간 있어요? Do you time?

네. 시간 있어요. Yes. I have time.

2.   What Number / How Many ~   몇 Counting Unit ~

몇 can be used in many different ways. 몇 is always followed by counting units.

You can also use this formula to ask the time.

Ex. 연필 몇 개 있어요? How many pencils do you have?

두 개 있어요. I have two.

개 몇 마리 있어요? How many dogs do you have?

세 마리 있어요. I have three.

몇   살 이에요? How old are you?

스물 다섯 살 이에요. I am 25 years old.

연습문제   Exercise

1. Please ask your partner the questions below and answer them.

    A. 교실에 사람   몇 명 있어요?

    B. 교실에 학생   몇 명 있어요?

    C. 교실에 선생님 몇 명 있어요?

    D. 교실에 남자   몇 명 있어요?

    E. 교실에 여자   몇 명 있어요?

2. Please ask your classmates' name and age in Korean and fill in the blanks below.

    Ex. 이름이 뭐예요?   에이미예요.

       몇 살 이에요?   스물 네 살 이에요.

이름	나이	이름	나이
에이미	24 (스물 네 살)	줄리앙	27 (스물 일곱 살)

3. Please ask your classmates about other people's age like the example below. Please use the chart that you made above.

    Ex. 에이미는 몇 살 이에요?   스물 네   살 이에요.

       줄리앙은 몇 살 이에요?   스물 일곱 살 이에요.

4. Please ask your classmate how many items there are like the example below.

> 사과 apple 3   연필 pencil 2   책 book 1
> 남자친구 boyfriend 4   여자친구 girlfriend 5   개 dog 2
> 와인 wine 6   핸드폰 cellphone 7

Ex. Q. 사과 몇 개 있어요?   A. 사과 세 개 있어요.

5. Please ask your classmates how many of the following nouns they have. Use the examples below and fill in the blanks.

Ex. 1   Q. 개 있어요?   A. 아니요. 없어요.

Ex. 2   Q. 펜 있어요?   A. 네. 있어요.

   Q. 펜 몇 개 있어요?   A. 다섯 개 있어요.

Ex. 3   Q. 물 있어요?   A. 네. 있어요.

   Q. 물 몇 병 있어요?   A. 열 한 병 있어요.

Ex. 4   Q. 친구 있어요?   A. 네. 있어요.

   Q. 친구 몇 명 있어요?   A. 일곱 명 있어요.

이름	친구 friend	펜 pen	개 dog	책 book	맥주 beer	물 water	
에이미	7	5	0	4	0	11	
	명	개	마리	권	병	잔	

Korean Signs You Should Recognize
알아두면 편리한 한국어 사인

You may see these signs a lot on the street. Please check out these signs using the internet or a dictionary and match.

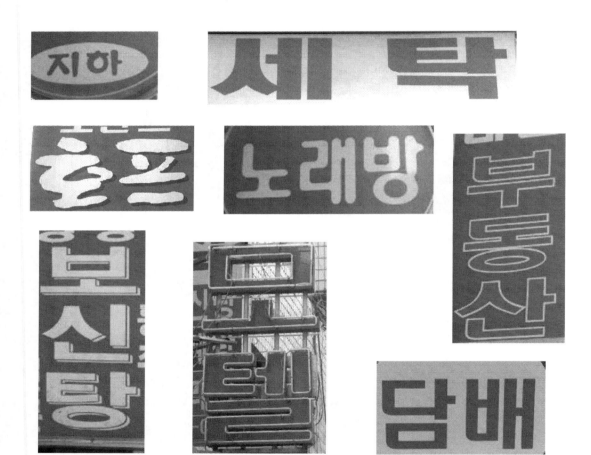

cigarette	dog meat stew
laundry	karaoke(singing room)
beer pub	underground, base
real estate agency	motel

제 4 과   맥주 얼마예요?

Lesson 4   How Much Is Beer?

1 USD = 1100 KRW

This is the exchange rate between US dollar and Korean won. $500 USD is ₩550,000 KRW. $30 USD is ₩33,000 KRW. This means that you will need to learn very high numbers. Discussing several hundred thousand is very common in Korea.

Let's go out and buy some beer for tonight while we practice our Chinese-based numbers!!

중요한 표현   Key Expressions

얼마예요?   How much is it?

몇 년생 이에요?   What year were you born in?

생일이 언제예요?   When is your birthday?

대화   Dialog

모건 : 맥주 얼마예요?

바텐더 : 오천 원 이에요.

모건 : 맥주 두 잔 주세요.

바텐더 : 그런데, 몇 년생 이에요?

모건 : 이천 삼 년 생 이에요.

바텐더 : 생일이 언제예요?

모건 : 십이 월 이십팔 일 이에요.

바텐더 : 그러면, 안돼요.

맥주 : beer   얼마예요? : how much is ~ ?

오천 : 5000 (Chinese number)

오천원 : 5000 won

두 : two (Korean number)   잔 : glass

주세요 : please give ,
        basic form "주다"   주다 : to give

그런데 : by the way

몇 : how many, what number

몇 년생 : what year of birth

이천 삼 : 2003 (Chinese number)

이천 삼 년 생 : year of birth (is) 2003

생일 : birthday   언제 : when

십이 : 12 (Chinese number)   월 : month

이십팔 : 28 (Chinese number)   일 : day

그러면 : then

안돼요 : to be impossible, not allowed

다양한 표현   More Expressions

지금 몇 시예요?   What time is it now?

오늘 며칠 이에요?   What date is it today?

안돼요.   It is (You are) not allowed. It is not possible.

괜찮아요.   It is all right.

발음   Pronunciation

맥주 [맥쭈]   오천원 [오처눤]   몇 년생 [면년생]
생일이 [생이리]   십이월 [시비월]

어휘   Vocabulary

1. 년   Year

Use Chinese numbers.

1978 천 구백 칠십 팔 년   2013 이천 십 삼 년

2. 월   Month

Use Chinese numbers.

January	February	March	April	May	June
일월(1월)	이월(2월)	삼월(3월)	사월(4월)	오월(5월)	유월(6월)

July	August	September	October	November	December
칠월(7월)	팔월(8월)	구월(9월)	시월(10월)	십일월(11월)	십이월(12월)

3. 일   Day

Use Chinese numbers.

1일(1st),   2일(2nd), 3일(3rd), ……30일(30st), 31일(31st)
일일   이일   삼일   삼십일   삼십일일

4. 시간   Time

You need to use Chinese numbers for minutes and Korean numbers for hours.

시	hour	분	minute
오전	before noon, AM	오후	afternoon, PM
새벽	early in the morning	아침	morning
저녁	evening	밤	night
1:30	한 시 삼십 분	12:00	열두 시
12:25	열두 시 이십 오 분	3:50	세 시 오십 분
11:39 AM	오전 열한 시 삼십 구 분	2:45 PM	오후 두 시 사십 오 분
5 in the morning	새벽 다섯 시	11 at night	밤 열한 시

문법   Grammar

1. When ~   언제 ~

생일이 언제예요?   When is your birthday?

한국어 수업이 언제예요?   When is the Korean class?

언제 한국에 왔어요?   When did you come to Korea?

2. Ordering an Item   Noun + 주세요

~ 주세요 means "Please give me ~ ". You can use this expression to order an item
that you want to buy.

Ex. 맥주 한 잔 주세요. Please give me a glass of beer.

   와인 세 병 주세요. Please give me three bottle of wine.

연습문제   Exercise

1. Please ask your class mates' birthday in Korean and fill in the blanks below.

 Ex. 생일이 언제예요?   십이 월 이십팔 일 이에요.

  몇 년생 이에요?   1982 (천 구백 팔십 이) 년생 이에요.

  몇 살 이에요?   32 (서른 두) 살 이에요.

이름 (name)	생일 (birthday)	출생 연도 (year of birth)	나이 (age)
모건	12월 28일	1982	32

2. Please ask your class mates about other people's birthday like the example below. Please use the chart that you made above.

 Ex. 모건은 생일이 언제예요?   십이 월 이십팔 일 이에요.

  모건은 몇 년생 이에요?   천 구백 팔십 이 년생 이에요.

  모건은 몇 살 이에요?   서른 두 살 이에요.

3. Please ask and answer the price of the items below and order them following the example below. You may change the underlined part.

맥주 beer (4,000 원)   맥북 Macbook (1,950,000 원)
와인 wine (8,500 원)   노트북 laptop (780,000 원)
소주 soju (3,000 원)   스마트폰 smartphone (538,000 원)
자전거 bicycle (251,300 원)   자동차 car (25,850,000 원)
볼펜 ball pen (500 원)   공책 notebook (1,500 원)
강아지 puppy (50,000 원)   고양이 cat (73,000 원)

Ex. A : <u>맥주</u> 얼마예요?

　　 B : <u>사천원(4000 won)</u> 이에요.

　　 A : <u>맥주 두 잔</u> 주세요.

　　 B : <u>팔천원(8000 won)</u> 이에요.

4. Please ask the time and answer in Korean.

Ex. 지금 몇 시예요?　　　오전 한 시 예요.

2:00　　3:45　　5:00　　<u>1:00 AM</u>　　2:30 PM　　10:45 AM　　11:25 PM

제 5 과　뭐 먹고 싶어요?

Lesson 5　What Do You Want to Eat?

What do you want to eat? Let's go out and eat something delicious. Please stop expecting your friends to order something for you. It is time for you to order what you want.

중요한 표현   Key Expressions

뭐 먹고 싶어요?   What do you want to eat?

소주 안 마시고 싶어요.   I don't want to drink soju.

대화   Dialog

앤디 : 뭐 먹고 싶어요?

혜민 : 삼겹살 먹고 싶어요.

앤디 : 밥도 먹고 싶어요?

혜민 : 네. 밥도 먹고 싶어요.

앤디 : 소주 마시고 싶어요?

혜민 : 소주 안 마시고 싶어요.

앤디 : 여기요!
　　　삼겹살 이 인분 하고
　　　공기밥 두 개 주세요.

뭐 : what

먹고 싶어요 : want to eat , basic form is "먹다"

먹다 : to eat

삼겹살 : Korean style pork belly bbq

밥 : rice   ~도 : also

소주 : soju

마시고 싶어요 : want to drink   basic form is "마시다"

마시다 : to drink

안 : not   안 마시고 싶어요 : do not want to drink

여기요! : here please! / hey! / come over here!

이 인분 : two portions of food

Noun-A 하고 Noun-B : Noun-A and Noun-B

공기밥 : a bowl of rice   두 개 : two things

주세요 : please give

다양한 표현   More Expressions

뭐 마시고 싶어요?   What do you want to drink?

어디 가고 싶어요?   Where do you want to go?

앞접시 주세요.   Please give me a small plate. (in a restaurant)

닭갈비 삼 인분 주세요.   Please give me three servings of bbq chicken.

발음   Pronunciation

먹고 [먹꼬]   싶어요 [시퍼요]   삼겹살 [삼겹쌀]
닭갈비 [닥깔비]   공기밥 [공기빱]

어휘   Vocabulary

1. Useful Vocabulary for This Chapter

식당	restaurant	술집	bar
반찬	side dish	밥	meal, rice(cooked)
메뉴	menu	컵	cup
물티슈	wet tissue	잔	glass
야채	vegetable	공기	rice bowl
고기	meat	젓가락	chopsticks
음료수	soda	숟가락	spoon
술	alcohol	물	water
먹다	to eat	마시다	to drink
가다	to go	어디	where
공부하다	to study	보다	to see
앞접시	small dish		

2. ~ 인분   Serving of Food

When you order some Korean food such as 부대찌개, 삼겹살, 갈비, 불고기, you need to order by the number of servings you want. You should use the Chinese number system.

삼겹살 오 인분   5 servings of samgyeopsal (Korean style bacon)
돼지갈비 삼 인분   3 servings of galbi (pork bbq)
불고기 이 인분   2 servings of bulgogi (marinated beef)

3. Examples of Counting Food and Drink

맥주, 소주, 와인   맥주 한 병 a bottle of beer   와인 두 잔 2 glasses of wine

소주 하나 a bottle of soju   소주 두 병 2 bottles of soju

김치찌개, 된장찌개   김치찌개 두 개 2 kimchi jjigaes

김치찌개 하나 1 kimchi jjigae

> 찌개 is a kind of stew.

된장찌개 삼 인분 3 servings of doengjang jjigae (soy bean stew)

피자   피자 세 개 3 pizzas   피자 두 판 2 pizzas

피자 한 조각 1 piece of pizza

피자 하나 1 pizza (1 piece or a whole pizza)

파스타, 햄버거   파스타 두 개 2 pastas   햄버거 한 개 1 burger

볶음밥, 비빔밥   볶음밥 한 개 1 fried rice   비빔밥 두 개 2 bibimbaps

비빔밥 하나 1 bimimbap

볶음밥 세 그릇 3 dishes of fried rice

비빔밥 두 그릇 2 dishes of bibimbap

김밥   김밥 세 개 3 kimbaps   김밥 하나 1 kimbap

김밥 두 줄 two rolls of kimbap

Note.   You usually can say "food/drink name 하나"

볶음밥 하나 1 fried rice   맥주 하나 1 beer   김치찌개 하나 1 kimchi stew

But, it is not natural to say "food/drink name 둘/셋/넷/ or more".

For two or more food/drinks, it is better say "food name 둘/셋/넷 or more + counting unit".

볶음밥 두 그릇 2 dishes of fried rice   맥주 다섯 잔 5 glasses of beer

문법   Grammar

1.   Want To ~   Verb Stem + 고 싶어요

This is used to indicate the desire of the subject. This pattern '~고 싶다' is used with first person statements and second person questions.

You just need to put ~고 싶어요 behind of the verb stem.

Stem	Ending		
마시	다	to drink	맥주 마시고 싶어요. I want to drink beer.
춤추	다	to dance	춤추고 싶어요. I want to dance.
먹	다	to eat	피자 먹고 싶어요? Do you want to eat pizza?
가	다	to go	한국에 가고 싶어요. I want to go to Korea.
			어디 가고 싶어요? Where do you want to go?
공부하	다	to study	뭐 공부하고 싶어요? What do you want to study?
하	다	to do	뭐 하고 싶어요? What do you want to do?

If you want to make negative meaning, you can put 안 in front of ~ 고 싶어요 or you can say ~고 싶지 않아요.

피자 안 먹고 싶어요. I don't want to eat pizza.

피자 먹고 싶지 않아요. I don't want to eat pizza.

2.   Noun-A and Noun-B   A 하고 B

피자 하고 콜라   pizza and cola   맥주 하고 소주   beer and soju

맥주 하고 소주 하고 칵테일 하고 위스키 마시고 싶어요.

                    I want to drink beer and soju and cocktail and whisky

3.   Where   어디

You can use 어디 to say where in English.

어디 가고 싶어요? Where do you want to go?

연습문제　Exercise

1. Please ask your classmates what they want to do as in the example below.
   Please use the phrases and vocabulary below.

   Ex. Q. 뭐 먹고 싶어요?　　　　　A. 피자 먹고 싶어요.

   　　Q. 어디에서 살고 싶어요?　　　A. 술집에서 살고 싶어요.

볶음밥 fried rice	불고기 bulgogi	피자 pizza
순두부 찌개 soft tofu stew	해물파전 green onion pancake with seafood	
소주 soju　커피 coffee	녹차 green tea	우유 milk
영화 movie　남자친구 boyfriend	여자친구 girlfriend	뮤지컬 musical
한국어 Korean　중국어 Chinese	수학 mathematics	토플 TOEFL
호텔 hotel　러브모텔 love motel		
찜질방 Korean style public bath/sauna	태국 Thailand	
제주도 Jeju Island　술집 bar	집 home, house	

   A. 뭐 먹고 싶어요?

   B. 뭐 마시고 싶어요?

   C. 뭐 보고 싶어요?

   D. 뭐 공부하고 싶어요?

   E. 어디 가고 싶어요?

   F. 어디에서 자고 싶어요?

   G. 어디에서 살고 싶어요?

   > ~에서 : at ~
   > 집에서 : at home
   > 제주도에서 : at (on) Jeju island
   > To learn more about ~에서,
   > please see page 64.

2. Please ask your classmates what they want to do as in the question list above
   and answer with multiple items. You can use your own vocabulary or the
   vocabulary above.

   Ex. Q. 어디 가고 싶어요?　　　A. 태국 하고 제주도 가고 싶어요.

   　　Q. 뭐 마시고 싶어요?　　　A. 물 하고 맥주 하고 소주 마시고 싶어요.

3. Imagine you are at a restaurant. Please ask your classmates what they want to eat and drink, and order food for them like the example below. You may change the underlined part

Ex.   A : 뭐 먹고 싶어요?

B : <u>닭갈비</u> 먹고 싶어요.

A : <u>맥주도</u> 마시고 싶어요?

B : 네. <u>맥주도</u> 마시고 싶어요.

A : 여기요! <u>맥주 한 병 하고 닭갈비 일 인분</u> 주세요.

볶음밥 fried rice   피자 pizza   순두부 찌개 soft tofu stew
비빔밥 bibimbap   제육덮밥 a bowl of rice topped with spicy pork
냉면 cold noodle   자장면 jajangmyeon, Chinese style black noodles
김밥 kimbap   닭갈비 dakgalbi (spicy grilled/bbq chicken)
돼지갈비 bbq pork   삼겹살 grilled pork belly
불고기 seasoned bbq beef   밥 rice
공기밥 a bowl of rice

소주 soju   맥주 beer   막걸리 milky rice wine
콜라 cola   물 water

전주 먹거리 여행
Eating Tour to Jeonju

Do you like Makkoli – Korean rice wine? Do you like Korean food?

If yes, Jeonju is a great place to visit to enjoy Makkoli and amazing Korean food. I will introduce a blog post about Makkoli and food trip to Jeonju.

Jeonju's Famous Cuisine and Too Much Makkoli

After going to the *hanok village* that I talked about in my first Jeonju post, we headed over to Makkoli Street (막걸리 골목) to find the famed makkoli restaurants that serve makkoli in kettles and provide an abundance of side dishes (안주) for each round of makkoli you order.

There is one very famous makkoli place around here, and we went there first, but because of the size of our group, we would have had to wait too long, so we decided to try the unknown instead.

Makkoli in Jeonju is a bit different from the Seoul type, we had two options; 맑은 막걸리 clear makkoli, or normal makkoli. Here on Makkoli Street, it's served three bottles at a time in kettles for about 12,000 won. Sound steep? Well, wait til you see all the side dishes that come along with the single order of Makkoli. I wouldn't suggest eating before you go (unless you really hate traditional Korean food, and I'm not talking kimbap cheonguk style, in which case fill up before you go because you might be disappointed with your options for food).

Our first makkoli joint turned out pretty good, but after two kettles, we decided to head out and check out another place. A sudden downpour made us pick a restaurant quick, but again, no disappointments. Their menu was similar but they sent out some of those strange Korean dishes

that should be on every foreigner's checklist to try before leaving: silkworm larvae, live octopus and fermented sashimi among others. I'll post about that later..

We had an early start, so we had a pretty early finish heading out around 11:30 to find a hotel to stay the night. Now, in Jeonju, if you want to stay at a nice place, like a hanok, you need to make reservations far in advance, BUT, if you want to stay in the cheapest possible place, then the (not so) little love motel area right behind the bus terminal is the place for you. We couldn't get a room at the first place we stopped at, but the second one was just perfect. 40,000 for the night with a jacuzzi. Despite bad connotations with love motels in other countries, love motels are not (very) sketchy and are generally fairly clean considering the price. Definitely an option for budget travelers here.

In the morning, we awoke with pretty bad hangovers and decided to find a restaurant to try the famous Jeonju 콩나물국밥 (beansprout soup and rice) which is, well, soup with beansprouts, rice and topped with an egg. Despite sounding bland and a little unappetizing, with a little red pepper powder added it was quite enjoyable.

Dinner on Sunday was the famous Jeonju Bibimbap.

Jeonju is well known for it's cuisine and if you ask any Korean they'll be able to list of things like bibimbap, bean sprout soup and makkoli as famous menu items here. While Jeonju may not be the most interesting place in Korea, it's cheap and interesting for a weekend getaway.

To see the original blog post, please visit here –
http://smileyjkl.blogspot.kr/2010/06/jeonjus-famous-cuisine-and-too-much.html

제 6 과   어디에서 데이트 해요?

Lesson 6   Where Do You Go on a Date?

~해요 is a magical verb.

Korean study 해요.	코리안 스터디 해요.	I study Korean.
Jogging 해요.	조깅 해요.	I jog.
Shopping 해요.	쇼핑 해요.	I go shopping.
Internet 해요.	인터넷 해요.	I use the internet.

중요한 표현 Key Expressions

한국어 수업 후에 뭐 해요? What do you do after Korean class?

어디에서 데이트 해요? Where do you go on a date?

홍대에 어떻게 가요? How do you go to Hongdae?

지하철로 가요. I go by subway.

대화   Dialog

알렉스 : 한국어 수업 후에 뭐 해요?	한국어 : Korean 수업 : class
	~ 후 : after ~ ~에 : at ~ 뭐 : what
	해요? : do? basic form is 하다
	하다 : to do
나디아 : 데이트 해요.	데이트 : date
	데이트해요 : go on a date
	데이트하다 : to go on a date
알렉스 : 어디에서 데이트 해요?	어디 : where ~에서 : at ~
나디아 : 홍대에서 데이트 해요.	홍대 : Hongik university, Hongdae area
알렉스 : 홍대에 어떻게 가요?	~에 : to ~ 어떻게 : how
	가요 : go basic form is 가다
나디아 : 지하철로 가요.	가다 : to go
	지하철 : subway ~(으)로 : by~

다양한 표현   More Expressions

오늘 뭐 해요? What do you do today?

주말에 뭐 해요? What do you do on the weekend?

걸어서 가요. I go by walking.

어휘   Vocabulary

1.   Magic Verb   ~하다

You can simply make a verb by put 하다 after a noun.

하다	to do		
일하다	to work	노래하다	to sing
공부하다	to study	인터넷하다	to use internet
식사하다	to have a meal	도착하다	to arrive
전화하다	to call (phone)	출발하다	to depart
운동하다	to exercise	시작하다	to start
애기하다	to talk	준비하다	to prepare
운전하다	to drive	연습하다	to practice
쇼핑하다	to go shopping	회의하다	to have a meeting
요리하다	to cook	데이트하다	to go on a date
여행하다	to travel	이사하다	to move
일하다	to work	블로그하다	to blog

You can easily adopt English adjectives as Korean by putting 하다 after the English adjectives.

쿨하다   to be cool   섹시하다   to be sexy

환타스틱하다   to be fantastic   핫하다   to be hot

When you want to say "It is delicious" in Korean, but if you don't know how to say "delicious" in Korean, just say "딜리셔스해요". It works.

Of course, many of these words are not academic.

2. Transportation   교통

자동차	car		자전거	bicycle
버스	bus		걸어서	on foot (walking)
지하철	subway		배	ship
택시	taxi		오토바이	motorbike
비행기	airplane		기차	train
트럭	truck			
~에	to ~		~(으)로	by ~ (transportation)

가다   to go   present tense : 가요

오다   to come   present tense : 와요

어떻게   how

한국어 수업에 어떻게 와요? How do you come to the Korean class?

지하철로 와요. I come by subway.

집에 어떻게 가요? How do you go home?

오토바이로 가요. I go by motorbike.

> To learn more about making present tense of verbs, please see page 70.

문법   Grammar

1. To Do ~   ~ 하다

하다 means to do. 하다 is conjugated to 해요 in the present tense.

Many nouns can be made into present tense verbs by adding the verb 해요.

일 (work)   + 해요 > 일해요   to work (verb)

공부 (study) + 해요 > 공부해요   to study (verb)

노래 (song) + 해요 > 노래해요   to sing (verb)

2. Negative Marker   안 + Verb

You can put 안 in front of most verbs to make it negative.

공부해요 > 공부 안 해요 I do not study

일해요 > 일 안 해요 I do not work

집에 가요 > 집에 안 가요 I don't go home

3. Cannot ~ / Not be good at ~   못 + Verb

If you put 못 in front of verbs, you can make the meaning of verb "cannot Verb"
or "not be good at doing Verb".

인터넷 해요 > 인터넷 못 해요 cannot use internet

연습해요 > 연습 못 해요 cannot practice

일해요 > 일 못 해요 cannot work/ not good at working

공부해요 > 공부 못 해요 cannot study / not good at studying

개고기 먹다 > 개고기 못 먹어요 cannot eat dog meat

4. Good at ~   잘 Verb ~

If you put 잘 in front of verb, it means "good at Verb-ing".

일 잘 해요? Are you good at doing work?

노래 잘 해요? Are you good at singing?

요리 잘 해요. I am good at cooking.

If you are not good at some something, you can yse 잘 못 ~

공부 잘 못 해요. I am not good at studying.

영어 잘 못 해요. I am not good at English.

5. Before/After + Noun   Noun + 전 / 후

7시 전에 뭐 해요? What do you do before 7 o'clock?

한국어 수업 전에 뭐 해요? What do you do before Korean class?

한국어 수업 후에 일해요. I work after Korean class.

퇴근 후에 뭐 해요? What do you do after work?

6. At a Location   Location + 에서

"*Location* + 에서"   means "at *Location*".

~에서 can be used before verbs except 있다/없다.

나는 학교에서 일해요. I work at a school.

어디에서 데이트해요? Where do you go on a date?

명동에서 쇼핑해요. I go shopping in Myeongdong.

나는 서울에서 살아요. I live in Seoul.

7. To a Location   Location + 에

With verbs like 가다 and 오다, "*Location* + 에" means "to *Location*".

홍대에 가요. I go to Hongdae.

어머니가 한국에 왔어요. My mother came to Korea.

8. By (means of) ~   ~(으)로

By putting (으)로 next to a transportation method, you can mean "by~".

Use ~로 for nouns ending with vowel, ~으로 for nouns ending with consonant.

홍대에 전철로 가요. I go to Hongdae by subway.

제주도에 비행기로 가요. I go to Jeju Island by airplane.

일본에 배로 가요. I go to Japan by boat.

연습문제   Exercise

1. Please see the pictures below and have a conversation like the example.

Ex. Q. 뭐 해요?   A. <u>요리 해요</u>.

      Q. <u>요리 잘 해요</u>?   A. 네. <u>요리 잘 해요</u>.

                                         아니요. <u>요리 잘 못 해요</u>.

> 공부하다 to study   운동하다 to exercise   노래하다 to sing
> 일하다 to work   운전하다 to drive   요리하다 to cook

2. Using the suggested vocabulary, please practice having a conversation like the example below.

Ex. Q. 한국어 수업 후에 공부해요?   A. 아니요. 공부 안 해요.

                                          네. 공부해요.

     Q. 출근 전에 샤워 해요?   A. 네. 샤워 해요.

                                          아니요. 샤워 안 해요.

> 출근 leaving home to go to work   퇴근 leaving the office after work
> 식사   meal   데이트 date   7시 7 o'clock
> ~ 전 before ~   ~ 후 after ~
> 회식하다 to have company dinner
> 샤워하다 to take shower   인터넷하다 to use the internet

제 6 과   어디에서 데이트 해요?

3. Using the suggested vocabulary, please practice having a conversation like the example below. You need to replace the underlined expressions.

Ex. Q. 어디에서 <u>공부해요</u>?   A. <u>집</u>에서 <u>공부해요</u>.

데이트하다 to go on a date   쇼핑하다 to go shopping
샤워하다   to take a shower   인터넷하다 to use the internet
일하다   to work   노래하다 to sing

홍대 Hongdae   모텔 motel   이태원 Itaewon
집 home   술집 bar   백화점 department store
이마트 E-Mart   인터넷 internet   학원 institute/academy
학교 school   회사 company
찜질방 Korean style public bath/ sauna

4. Using the suggested vocabulary, please practice having a conversation like the example below. You need to replace the underlined expressions.

Ex. Q. <u>홍대</u>에 어떻게 가요?   A. <u>전철로</u> 가요.
   Q. <u>집</u>에 어떻게 가요?   A. <u>걸어서</u> 가요.

미국 USA   중국 China   일본 Japan
캐나다 Canada   멕시코 Mexico   제주도 Jeju Island
부산 Busan   집 home
강남역 Gangnam station

기차 train   지하철 subway, underground
전철 subway, metro   버스 bus   택시 taxi
자전거 bicycle   비행기 airplane   배 ship
오토바이 motorbike   걸어서 on foot, by walking

제 7 과   우리, 같이 인도 음식 먹어요!

Lesson 7   Let's Eat Indian Food Together!

인도 음식 먹어요.   I eat Indian food.

인도 음식 먹어요.   Let's eat Indian food.

인도 음식 먹어요.   Eat Indian food!

인도 음식 먹어요?   Do you eat Indian food?

What?? Well, it is quite simple. Isn't it?

It is time to learn how to conjugate verbs to the present tense.

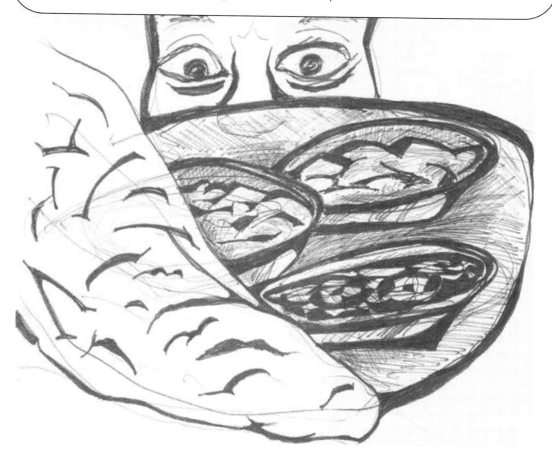

중요한 표현   Key Expressions

인도 음식 좋아해요?   Do you like Indian food?

같이 술 마셔요.   Let's have a drink together.

대화   Dialog

제프 : 인도 음식 좋아해요?

인도 : India   음식 : food

좋아해요 : like   basic form is 좋아하다

좋아하다 : to like

덴　 : 네, 좋아해요.

　　　제프 씨는 어때요?

어때요? : how about ~

제프 : 저도 인도 음식을 좋아해요.

저 : I, polite form   ~도 : ~ also

덴　 : 우리, 같이 인도 음식 먹어요!

우리 : we   같이 : together

먹어요 : eat   basic form is 먹다   먹다 : to eat

제프 : 좋아요.

좋아요 : good   basic form is 좋다   좋다 : to be good

다양한 표현   More Expressions

같이 저녁 먹어요.   Let's eat dinner together.

나는 채식주의자예요.   I am a vegetarian.

고기 빼고 주세요.   Please give it to me without meat.

소주는 그냥 그래요.   Soju is just so so.

발음   Pronunciation

같이 [가치]   좋아요 [조아요]   좋아해요 [조아해요]

먹어요 [머거요]   읽어요 [일거요]

어휘   Vocabulary

1. Verbs   동사

Basic Form		Present Tense
있다	to exist/to have	있어요
없다	not to exist/not to have	없어요
자다	to sleep	자요
일어나다	to get up	일어나요
보다	to see/look/watch	보아요 > 봐요
놀다	to play	놀아요
먹다	to eat	먹어요
마시다	to drink	마시어 요 > 마셔요
주다	to give	주어요 > 줘요
가다	to go	가요
오다	to come	오아요 > 와요
사다	to buy	사요
배우다	to learn	배우어요 > 배워요
가르치다	to teach	가르치어요 > 가르쳐요
만나다	to meet	만나요
읽다	to read	읽어요
쉬다	to rest	쉬어요
만들다	to make	만들어요
빌리다	to borrow	빌리어요 > 빌려요
찾다	to find	찾아요
쓰다	to use, to write	쓰어요 > 써요
받다	to get/receive	받아요
살다	to live	살아요
좋다	to be good	좋아요
좋아하다	to like	좋아해요

문법   Grammar

1. Present Tense   ~어요/아요/해요

~어요 / 아요 / 해요 form is the informal polite present tense.

A. ~하다 > 해요

좋아하다 > 좋아해요

공부하다 > 공부해요

B. Verb stem, ending with ㅏ or ㅗ + 아요

가다 > 가 + 아요 > 가요

놀다 > 놀 + 아요 > 놀아요

오다 > 오 + 아요 > 와요

좋다 > 좋 + 아요 > 좋아요

살다 > 살 + 아요 > 살아요

C. Verb stem of other verbs + 어요

먹다 > 먹 + 어요 > 먹어요

만들다 > 만들 + 어요 > 만들어요

2. Object marker   Noun + 을/를

To indicate the object, you can put 을 or 를 behind the object.

Please note this object marker is easily omitted in conversational Korean.

You use 을 for words ending with consonant, 를 for words ending with vowel.

Ex. 인도 음식을 좋아해요? Do you like Indian food?

저는 한국어를 공부해요. I study Korean.

3. Making suggestions "let's ~ "   같이 + Present Tense

같이 영화 봐요. Let's watch a movie together.

같이 밥 먹어요. Let's have a meal together.

To emphasize the suggestion, you can add 우리 in front of the phrase.

우리, 같이 술 마셔요. Let's have a drink together.

우리, 같이 공부해요. Let's study together.

4. How about Noun?   Noun + 은/는 어때요?

This expression is to ask other people's opinion about something or someone already mentioned during conversation.

A : 이 셔츠가 예뻐요. This shirt is pretty.

B : 저 옷은 어때요? How about those clothes?

A : 토요일에 시간 있어요? Do you have time on Saturday?

B : 아니요. 없어요. 금요일은 어때요? No, I don't. How about Friday?

5. To Like Vs. To Be Good   좋아하다 Vs. 좋다

Basic Form	Present Tense	Marker (you can omit it)
좋아하다 to like	좋아해요	~을/를 (object marker)
김치찌개를 좋아해요. I like kimchi stew. 나를 좋아해요? Do you like me? 인도음식 좋아해요. I like Indian food.		
좋다 to be good (to like)	좋아요	~이/가 (subject marker) ~은/는 (topic marker)
오늘 날씨가 좋아요. Today's weather is good. 인도음식은 좋아요. Indian food is good. (I like Indian food.) 맥주 좋아요. Beer is good. (I like beer.)		

제 7 과   우리, 같이 인도 음식 먹어요!

연습문제   Exercise

1. Please change suggested verbs to ~어요/아요 form and ask a question using 뭐.
   Please answer using the suggested vocabulary.

   Ex. Q. 먹다 > 뭐 먹어요?   A. 피자 먹어요.

   Q. 마시다 > 뭐 마셔요?   A. 물 마셔요.

보다 to see	먹다 to eat	마시다 to drink
좋아하다 to like	읽다 to read	만들다 to make
사다 to buy	필요하다 to need, to be necessary	

영화 movie	뮤지컬 musical	뮤직비디오 music video
파스타 pasta	라면 ramen	볶음밥 fried rice
맥주 beer	주스 juice	와인 wine
책 book	소설 novel	신문 newspaper
스마트폰 smartphone	인터넷 internet	컴퓨터 computer

2. Please change the suggested verbs to ~어요/아요 form and ask a question using 언제 and an object marker 을/를. Please answer using the suggested vocabulary.

Ex. Q. 먹다 > 언제 저녁을 먹어요?   A. 7시에 저녁을 먹어요.

    Q. 마시다 > 언제 술을 마셔요?   A. 아침에 술을 마셔요.

선물 gift	선생님 teacher	친구 friend
애인 lover	빵 bread	케익 cake
책 book	한국어 Korean	요가 yoga
아침 morning, breakfast	오전 before noon	오후 afternoon
점심 lunch, lunch time	저녁 evening	밤 night
7시 (일곱시) 7 o'clock	10시 (열시) 10 o'clock	5시 25분 (다섯 시 이십 오 분)
크리스마스 Christmas	생일 birthday	

A. 주다

B. 만나다

C. 만들다

D. 읽다

E. 사다

F. 배우다

클럽 club (dance club)	제주도 Jeju Island	부산 Busan
영화 movie	뮤지컬 musical	티브이 TV
맥주 beer	칵테일 cocktail	커피 coffee
막걸리 makgeoli, rice wine		소주 soju
한국어 Korean	스페인어 Spanish	중국어 Chinese
요가 yoga	골프 golf	수영 swimming
오바마 Obama	김정은 Kim Jeong Eun	소녀시대 girl's generation
트럼프 Trump	데니스 로드만 Dennis Rodman	

가다 to go	보다 to see	마시다 to drink
배우다 to learn	만나다 to meet	

3. Using the vocabulary above, please practice having a conversation like the example below. You need to replace the underlined expressions.

   Ex. A : <u>와인</u> 좋아해요?

   　　B : 네. <u>와인</u> 좋아해요.

   　　A : 우리, 같이 <u>와인 마셔요</u>.

   　　B : 좋아요. 같이 <u>와인 마셔요</u>.

4. Using the suggested vocabulary above, please practice having a conversation, as in the example below. You need to replace the underlined expressions.

   Ex. A : 우리, 같이 <u>와인 마셔요</u>.

   　　B : <u>와인</u>은 그냥 그래요.

   　　A : <u>맥주</u>는 어때요?

   　　B : 좋아요. 같이 <u>맥주 마셔요</u>.

제 8 과   머리하고 목이 아파요.

Lesson 8   My Head and Throat Hurt.

Don't be sick. It is depressing to be sick in a foreign country.
But, if you are sick, you'd better know your body parts and several symptoms to explain to your doctor.

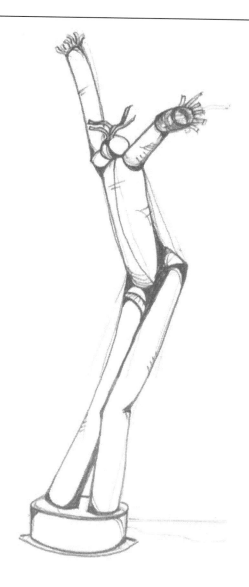

중요한 표현 Key Expressions

머리하고 목이 아파요.   I have a headache and a sore throat.

괜찮아요.   That's all right/ I'm all right.

대화   Dialog

채드 : 어디가 아파요?   어디 : where   ~가 : subject marker

                             아파요 : hurt   basic form is "아프다 : to hurt"

상현 : 머리하고 목이 아파요.   머리 : head   목 : neck, throat

                             머리 하고 목 : head and throat

                             ~이 : subject marker

채드 : 열 있어요?   열 : fever   있다 : to have, to exist

                             있어요? : do you have?   basic form is "있다"

상현 : 열 조금 있어요.   조금 : a little

채드 : 병원에 가세요.   병원 : hospital, clinic   ~에 : to ~

                             가세요 : please go   basic form is "가다"

                             가다 : to go

상현 : 괜찮아요. 약 있어요.   괜찮아요 : it is okay   basic form is "괜찮다"

                             괜찮다 : to be okay, to be all right   약 : medicine

다양한 표현   More Expressions

열 나요.   I have a fever.

감기 걸렸어요.   I caught a cold.

기침 조금 해요.   I have a small cough.

발음   Pronunciation

목이 [모기]   있어요 [이써요]   병원에 [병워네]   괜찮아요 [괜차나요]

어휘   Vocabulary

1. 신체 부위   Parts of the Body

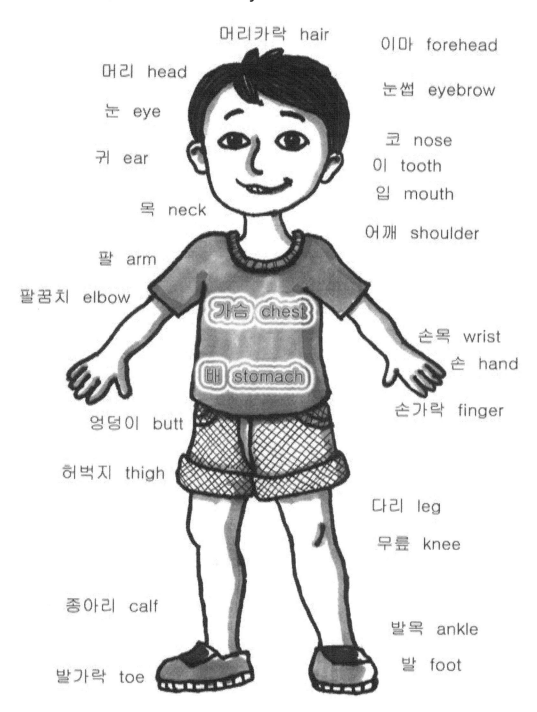

머리카락 hair

이마 forehead

머리 head

눈썹 eyebrow

눈 eye

코 nose

귀 ear

이 tooth

입 mouth

목 neck

어깨 shoulder

팔 arm

팔꿈치 elbow

가슴 chest

손목 wrist

손 hand

배 stomach

손가락 finger

엉덩이 butt

허벅지 thigh

다리 leg

무릎 knee

종아리 calf

발목 ankle

발 foot

발가락 toe

제 8 과   머리하고 목이 아파요.

2. 의료 용어   Medical Vocabulary

아프다	to hurt	~ 아파요	~ hurts.
목 아파요.	My neck/throat hurts.	머리 아파요.	My head hurts.
병원	hospital, clinic	약국	pharmacy
의사	doctor	간호사	nurse
약	medicine		
감기	cold	감기 걸렸어요	I caught a cold.
열	fever	열 나다	to have a fever
기침	cough	기침 하다	to cough
많이	a lot (adverb)	조금	a little (adverb)
내과	internal medicine clinic	피부과	dermatology clinic (skin clinic)
외과	surgical clinic	안과	ophthalmology (eye clinic)
치과	dental clinic	이비인후과	earn nose and throat doctor
산부인과	obstetrics and gynecology	응급실	emergency room
성형외과	plastic surgery clinic	한의원	Korean (oriental) clinic

문법   Grammar

1. Noun-A and Noun-B   Noun-A 하고 Noun-B

머리 하고 목   head and throat   손 하고 발   hands and feet

머리하고 목하고 손이 아파요. My head, throat and hands hurt.

배하고 다리가 아파요. My stomach and legs hurt.

2. Verb and ~   Verb Stem 고 ~

먹다 + 마시다 > 먹고 마시다 > 먹고 마셔요. I eat and drink.

피자를 먹다 + 맥주를 마시다 > 피자를 먹고 맥주를 마셔요.

I eat pizza and drink beer.

머리가 아프다 + 열이 나다 > 머리가 아프고 열이 나요.

I have a headache and a fever.

78

연습문제   Exercise

1. Please ask and answer about your body part like the example below. You need to replace the underlined expressions.

   Ex.   A: 이거 뭐예요?   (Please point a part of your body)

   B: 머리예요.

   A: 머리 몇 개 있어요?

   B: 한 개 있어요.

2. Please ask where it hurts and talk about what clinic you should go like the example below. You need to replace the underlined expressions.

   Ex.   A: 어디가 아파요?

   B: 코 아파요.

   A: 어떤 병원에 가요?

   B: 이비인후과에 가요.

3. Please ask where it hurts. Please answer with more than two body part using 하고 like the example below. You need to replace the underlined expressions.

   Ex.   Q. 어디가 아파요?   A. 머리하고 배가 아파요.

4. Please ask where it hurts. Please answer with more than two symptoms using ~고 like the example below. You need to replace the underlined expressions.

   Ex.   Q. 어디가 아파요?   A. 머리가 아프고 열이 나요.

5. Please match the symptom and what you should do. You can choose multiple options.

A. 머리가 아파요   내과에 가요

B. 열 나요   약을 먹어요

C. 목이 아파요   약국에 가요

D. 눈이 아파요   치과에 가요

E. 이가 아파요   성형외과에 가요

F. 못생겼어요   이비인후과에 가요

G. 귀하고 목이 아파요   집에서 쉬어요

                                        안과에 가요

제 9 과   내일 뭐 할 거예요?

Lesson 9   What Will You Do Tomorrow?

Is there someone you like? Does he/she also like you? If not, let's stalk them by asking their plans. Of course you should use the future tense.

In case someone is stalking you, you should also know how to turn down annoying questions.

중요한 표현 Key Expressions

내일 뭐 할 거예요? What will you do tomorrow?

저녁 먹을 거예요. I will eat dinner.

대화 Dialog

줄리앙 : 내일 뭐 할 거예요?

내일 : tomorrow   뭐 : what

하다 : to do

할 거예요? : will do?   basic form "하다"

에이미 : 이태원에 갈 거예요.

~에 : to~   가다 : to go

갈 거예요 : will go   basic form "가다"

줄리앙 : 이태원에서 뭐 할 거예요?

~에서 : at~

> To learn more about ~에 and ~에서, please see page 64.

에이미 : 저녁 먹을 거예요.

저녁 : dinner

먹을 거예요 : will eat, basic form "먹다"

줄리앙 : 뭐 먹을 거예요?

먹다 : to eat   뭐 : what

에이미 : 멕시코 음식 먹을 거예요.

멕시코 : Mexico   음식 : food

줄리앙 : 누구랑 먹을 거예요?

누구 : who   ~(이)랑 : with~

에이미 : 알 거 없어요.

알 거 없어요 : you don't need to know.

다양한 표현   More Expressions

몰라도 돼요. You don't need to know.

신경 끄세요. Mind your own business.

발음   Pronunciation

할 거예요 [할 꺼예요]   이태원에 [이태워네]   먹을 [머글]

어휘   Vocabulary

1. 날짜의 표현

그저께	the day before yesterday	어제	Yesterday
오늘	today	내일	Tomorrow
모레	the day after tomorrow		

오늘 친구 만날 거예요. I will meet a friend today.

내일 맥주 마실 거예요. I will drink beer tomorrow.

1월 5일 (일월 오일) January 5th   8월 27일 (팔월 이십칠일) August 27th

10월 8일 (시월 팔일) October 8th   6월 15일 (유월 십오일) June 15th

1월 5일에 부산 갈 거예요. I will go to Busan on January 5th.

10월 8일에 영화 볼 거예요. I will watch a movie on October 8th.

~에   at/in/on ~   (time expression)

1월 5일에   on January 5th   생일에   on a birthday

크리스마스에   on Christmas   3시에   at 3 o'clock

5월에   in May

> Please note that you don't use ~에 for 그저께, 어제, 오늘, 내일 모레.

문법   Grammar

1. Future Tense   Verb Stem + ㄹ / 을 거예요

It's the simple future tense. It can be used for both statements and questions.

A. Verb stem, ending with vowel + ㄹ 거예요

보다 > 오늘 영화 볼 거예요. I will watch a movie today.

공부하다 > 내일 공부할 거예요? Will you study tomorrow?

B. Verb stem, ending with ㄹ + 거예요

놀다 > 내일 친구랑 놀 거예요. I will hang out with friends tomorrow.

C. Verb stem, ending with other under-consonant + 을 거예요.

먹다 > 멕시코 음식을 먹을 거예요. I will eat Mexican food.

연습문제   Exercise

1. Please ask your classmates about their plans like the example below. Please use the vocabulary in the box.

   Ex. Q. 내일 뭐 할 거예요?   What will you do tomorrow?

   A. 영화 볼 거예요.   I will watch a movie.

크리스마스 Christmas   석가탄신일 Buddha's Birthday   어린이날 Children's day
근로자의 날 Labor's day   설날 Lunar new year   추석 Full moon day
생일 birthday   주말 weekend   휴가 vacation/holiday

가다 to go
도서관 library   공원 park   백화점 department store
시장 market   제주도 Jeju island

만나다 to meet
친구 friend 선생님 teacher 애인 lover 아버지 father 어머니 mother

공부하다 to study
한국어 Korean 스페인어 Spanish 중국어 Chinese 영어 English

보다 to see
영화 movie   뮤지컬 musical   오페라 opera

먹다 to eat
아침 breakfast   점심 lunch   저녁 dinner   브런치 brunch
개고기 dog meat 파스타 pasta 샐러드 salad 케밥 kebab

마시다 to drink
커피 coffee 맥주 beer 물 water 주스 juice 와인 wine

2. Please stalk your classmates like the example below.

A: 주말에 뭐 할 거예요?   What will you do on the weekend?

B: 와인 마실 거예요.   I will drink wine.

A: <u>어디에서</u> 마실 거예요?   Where will you drink?

B: <u>집에서</u> 마실 거예요.   I will drink at home.

A: <u>누구랑</u> 마실 거예요?   With whom will you drink?

B: <u>친구랑</u> 마실 거예요.   I will drink with a friend.

A: <u>어떤</u> 친구랑 마실 거예요?   With what kinds of friends will you drink?

B: 몰라도 돼요.   You don't need to know.

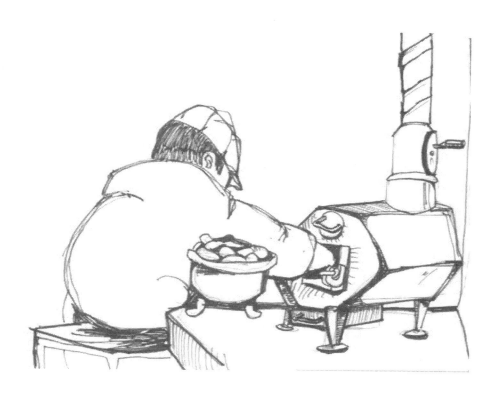

4대강 자전거 여행

4 Rivers Cross-Country Bicycle Road Tour

Bike path along the North Han River

If you happen to be a cyclist in Korea, you may have already realized that you've hit the jackpot. Without much fanfare, Korea has been developing its bike paths over the past few years, particularly through the 4 rivers project, and it is now possible to ride on beautiful bike paths around the country. It's the perfect way to take in Korea's beautiful scenery without having to deal with tour companies, traffic on highways, or overwhelming numbers of tourists at the top destinations around the country.

If the power compels you, you can start in Incheon at the Ara sea lock and ride all the way down to Busan, a total of 633km. But, for those who aren't ready for a week or more of intense bike riding, anyone can take advantage, either by taking your own bike for a day trip or by renting bikes at many free bike rental stations. To rent a bike, just be sure to bring proper identification!

While on the paths, you'll discover that they are, for the most part, very well maintained with plenty of signage, often in both English and Korean so you will hopefully never get lost!

The terrain differs from trail to trail, but as most of the trails follow the rivers closely, you'll find that it rarely gets difficult. Occasionally, the paths stray off the rivers and that's when you might find yourself on a steep hill or following a road with car traffic. However, these roads tend to be country roads with few cars .

Another neat feature of certain trails is how they have been converted from their original uses. Several trails were once train routes. It was pretty ingenious of them to convert these old tracks into bike paths. The flat land was already there, and so were the tunnels! It can be really refreshing to pass through one of these cool (both temperature- and interest-wise) tunnels when biking through the hot summer heat!

For those who are interested in biking a lot, the most rewarding way to do it is to buy yourself a 'passport' to the 4 Rivers Cross-Country Cycling Road Tour. As

Standing In line to stamp a passport

you ride along the paths, you will occasionally pass signs that look like the one above. These indicate that a 'certification point' is coming up soon. A 'certification Center' is where, if you have a 'passport' you can stamp your passport to show your biking achievements.

Certification centers look like the British red telephone boxes. They're usually hard to miss, but if you don't know it's coming up (like if you miss the sign) you could miss it, so be sure to keep your eyes open! Inside you'll find a stamp and ink pad. Be sure to mark the right spot!

Passports can be purchased at many places around the 4 rivers cycling paths. Many bike cafes and repair shops sell them, plus some official certification centers.

Where to start? Anywhere! If you are living in Seoul, then the Han River would be an ideal place to go. Beginners to long distance biking may like to just start biking the length of the Han River in Seoul, or maybe going to the end of the Ara Canal in Incheon. However, as these paths criss-cross the country, and many towns and cities have their own bike paths which are not affiliated with the 4 rivers project, there is no excuse not to give biking in Korea a try!

For more information, please visit their official web site –
http://www.riverguide.go.kr/eng/index.do

제 10 과   토요일에 뭐 했어요?

Lesson 10   What Did You Do on Saturday?

Ask what your boyfriend ate for lunch.

Ask who your girlfriend met last weekend.

Ask where your future ex-boyfriend went yesterday.

Ask when your ex-girlfriend got a new boyfriend.

중요한 표현   Key Expressions

토요일에 뭐 했어요?   What did you do on Saturday?

집에서 잤어요.   I slept at home.

백화점에서 쇼핑했어요.   I shopped at a department store.

대화   Dialog

줄리앙 : 토요일에 뭐 했어요?

토요일 : Saturday

~에 : on/at/in ~   뭐 : what

했어요 : did ,   basic form "하다"   하다 : to do

에이미 : 집에서 쉬었어요.

집 : home   ~에서 : on/at/in ~

쉬었어요 : rested   basic form "쉬다"

쉬다 : to rest

줄리앙 : 남자친구랑 같이 있었어요?

남자친구 : boyfriend

~(이)랑 : with ~   같이 : together

있었어요 : existed, had   basic form "있다"

있다 : to have, to exist

에이미 : 아니요. 혼자 있었어요.

혼자 : alone

줄리앙 : 혼자 뭐 했어요?

에이미 : 영화 보고 밥 먹고 잤어요.

영화 : movie   보고 : watch and ~

밥 : meal   먹고 : eat and ~

잤어요 : slept   basic form "자다"

자다 : to sleep

줄리앙 : 재미있었어요?

재미있었어요 : was fun/interesting

재미있다 : to be fun, interesting

에이미 : 아니요. 심심했어요.

심심했어요 : was bored   basic form "심심하다"

심심하다 : to be bored

다양한 표현   More Expressions

제발 그만 하세요. Please stop (doing something annoying.)

하지 마! Please stop!

물어보지 마세요. Please don't ask.

발음   Pronunciation

토요일에 [토요이레]   쉬었어요 [쉬어써요]   같이 [가치]

했어요 [해써요]   재미있었어요 [재미이써써요]

보고 [보고]   먹고 [먹꼬]

어휘   Vocabulary

1. 요일의 표현   Days of the Week

월요일	Monday	화요일	Tuesday
수요일	Wednesday	목요일	Thursday
금요일	Friday	토요일	Saturday
일요일	Sunday		
지난주	last week	이번주	this week
다음주	next week		
주중	weekday	주말	weekend
지난 주말	last weekend	이번 주말	this weekend
다음 주말	next weekend		
~에	on/at/in ~		

To know more about ~에, please see page 64.

월요일에 뭐 했어요? What did you do on Monday?

지난 주말에 뭐 했어요? What did you do last weekend?

다음주 토요일에 뭐 할 거예요? What will you do next Saturday?

문법   Grammar

1. **Past Tense**   **Verb Stem + ㅆ어요/ 었어요 / 았어요 / 했어요**

This is the polite past tense. It can be used for both statements and questions.

A. Verb stem, ending with ㅏ/ ㅓ / ㅐ / ㅔ (without final consonant) + ㅆ어요

가다 > 학교에 갔어요? Did you go to school?

서다 > 섰어요. I stood up.

깨다 > 접시를 깼어요. I broke a dish.

B. Verb stem, ending with ㅏ (with final consonant)

　　　　　 or ㅗ (with or without final consonant) + 았어요

알다 > 알았어요. I knew it. / I got it.

높다 > 빌딩이 너무 높았어요. The building was too high.

C. ~하다 > ~했어요.

숙제하다 > 숙제했어요. I did homework.

D. Other verb stem + 었어요

먹다 > 피자를 먹었어요. I ate pizza.

2. **Connecting Verbs**   **Verb Stem A + 고 + Verb B**

"Verb-A stem + 고 + Verb-B" means "Verb-A and Verb-B".

Please note that you need to conjugate the last verb only.

Ex. 마시다 + 먹다 > 마시고 먹었어요   drank and ate

영화 보다 + 밥 먹다 + 자다 > 영화 보고 밥 먹고 잤어요.

　　　　　　　　　　 I watched a movie and ate a meal and slept.

연습문제   Exercise

1. Please ask your classmates what they did on various days of the week like the example below. Please use the suggested verbs in the box.

   Ex. 월요일에 뭐 했어요?   What did you do on Monday?

   　　집에서 일했어요.   I worked at home.

화요일 Tuesday	목요일 Thursday
주말 weekend	지난 주말 last weekend
지난주 last week	지난주 금요일 last Friday

놀다 to hang out	**싸우다 to fight**	**자다 to sleep**
친구랑 with friends	강아지랑 with a puppy	
여자친구랑 with (my) girlfriend		
집에서 at home	공원에서 in the park	모텔에서 at a motel

가르치다 to teach	**배우다 to learn**	**공부하다 to study**
영어 English	한국어 Korean	중국어 Chinese
학교에서 at a school	복지관에서 at a community center	
도서관에서 at a library		

읽다 to read		
잡지 magazine	신문 newspaper	소설 novel

2. Please ask your classmates what they did on various days of the week like the example below. Please use as many of the verbs above as you can.

   Ex. 화요일에 뭐 했어요?   What did you do on Tuesday?

   　　친구랑 싸우고 소주 마시고 집에서 잤어요.

   　　　　　I fought with a friend, drank soju and slept at home.

Dialog Translation
대화 번역

Lesson 1

Haemin	Hello. Glad to meet you.
Molly	Hi. What is your name?
Haemin	I am Haemin.
Molly	I am Molly.
Haemin	Where are you from?
Molly	I am American.

Lesson 2

Mathew	What is this?
Soyoung	This is a book.
Mathew	What kind of book is this?
Soyoung	It is a Korean language book.
Mathew	Whose is this?
Soyoung	It is Andy's.
Mathew	Who is Andy?
Soyoung	That person.

Lesson 3

Amy	How old are you?
Julien	I am 27 years old.
Amy	I am 24 years old.
Julien	Do you a boyfriend?
Amy	Yes. I have.
Julien	How many boyfriends do you have?
Amy	I have 3.

Lesson 4

Morgan	How much is beer?
Bartender	It is 5000 won.
Morgan	Please give me 2 glasses of beer.
Bartender	By the way, what year were you born?
Morgan	I was born in 2003.
Bartender	When is your birthday?
Morgan	It is December 28th.
Bartender	Then, I cannot.

Lesson 5

Andy	What do you want to eat?
Haemin	I want to eat Korean style pork belly bbq.
Andy	Do you want to eat rice also?
Haemin	Yes. I want to eat rice too.
Andy	Do you want to drink soju?
Haemin	I don't want to drink soju.
Andy	Here! Please give me 2 potion of pork belly bbq and 2 bowls of rice.

Lesson 6

Alex	What do you do after the Korean class?
Nadia	I go on a date.
Alex	Where do you go on a date?
Nadia	I date in Hongdae.
Alex	How do you go to Hongdae?
Nadia	I go by subway.

Lesson 7

Jeff	Do you like Indian food?
Den	Yes. I like. How about you?
Jeff	I also like Indian food.
Den	Let's eat Indian food together.
Jeff	Good.

Lesson 8

Chad	Where does it hurt?
Sanghyun	My head and throat hurt.
Chad	Do you have fever?
Sanghyun	I have a little fever.
Chad	Go to a clinic.
Sanghyun	It is okay. I have a medicine.

Lesson 9

Julien	What will you do tomorrow?
Amy	I will go to Itaewon.
Julien	What will you do in Itaewon?
Amy	I will eat dinner.
Julien	What will you eat?
Amy	I will eat Mexican food.
Julien	With whom will you eat?
Amy	You don't need to know.

Dialog Translation

Lesson 10

Julien	What did you do on Saturday?
Amy	I rested at home.
Julien	Were you with your boyfriend?
Amy	No. I was alone.
Julien	What did you do by yourself?
Amy	I watched a movie, ate meal and slept.
Julien	Was it fun?
Amy	No. It was boring.

흥인지문 Heung In Ji Mun - East Main Gate of Seoul Fortress

Exercise Answer Key
연습문제 정답

Please note that this answer key is suggested for your reference.

Please try to be creative and make your own answers.

제 1 과 저는 혜민이에요.

1	A.	저는 상현이에요.	I am Sanghyun.
	B.	저는 영숙이에요.	I am Yeongsook.
	C.	저는 스테파니예요.	I am Stephanie.
	D.	저는 에이미예요.	I am Amy.
2	A.	마이클 잭슨은 미국사람이에요.	Michael Jackson is American.
	B.	브루스 리는 홍콩사람이에요.	Bruce Lee is from Hong Kong.
	C.	스탈린은 러시아사람이에요.	Stalin is Russian.
	D.	휴 그랜트는 영국사람이에요.	Hugh Grant is English.

3 Please exercise conversation with other people.

4 Please exercise conversation with other people.

5 Please exercise conversation with other people.

제 2 과 저는 혜민이에요.

1 Please exercise conversation with other people.

2	A.	이 지갑은 누구 거예요?	Whose is this wallet?
		그건 마이크 거예요.	It is Mike's.
	B.	저건 누구 신발이에요?	Whose shoes are those?
		그건 스테파니 거예요.	It is Stephanie's.
	C.	이건 누구 거예요?	Whose is this?
		그건 제 신발이에요.	It is my shoes.
	D.	이 핸드폰은 누구거예요?	Whose is this cellular phone?
		그건 줄리앙 거예요.	It is Julien's.
3	A.	이게 무슨 음악이에요?	What kind of music is this?
		팝송 이에요.	It is a pop song.
	B.	이게 무슨 영화예요?	What kind of movie is this?
		액션영화예요.	It is an action movie.
	C.	이게 무슨 음식이에요?	What kind of food is this?
		돼지갈비예요.	It is Korean style pork bbq.

제 3 과 남자친구 몇 명 있어요?

1 A. 교실에 사람 몇 명 있어요?   How many people are there in the classroom?
       열 명 있어요.   There are 10 people.

   B. 교실에 학생 몇 명 있어요?   How many students are there in the classroom?
       아홉 명 있어요.   There are 9 students.

   C. 교실에 선생님 몇 명 있어요. How many teachers are there in the classroom?
       한 명 있어요.   There is 1 teacher.

   D. 교실에 남자 몇 명 있어요?   How many men are there in the classroom?
       다섯 명 있어요.   There are 5 men.

   E. 교실에 여자 몇 명 있어요?   How many women are there in the classroom?
       네 명 있어요.   There are 4 women.

2 A. 상현은 몇 살 이에요?   How old is Sanghyun?
       열아홉 살 이에요.   He is 19 years old.

   B. 줄리앙은 몇 살 이에요?   How old is Julien?
       스물 일곱 살 이에요.   He is 27 years old.

3 A. 이름이 뭐예요?   What is your name?
       상현이에요.   I am Sanghyun.
       몇 살 이에요?   How old are you?
       열아홉 살 이에요.   I am 19 years old.

4 A. 사과 몇 개 있어요?   How many apples do you have?
       세 개 있어요.   I have three.

   B. 연필 몇 개 있어요?   How many pencils do you have?
       두 개 있어요.   I have two.

   C. 책 몇 권 있어요?   How many books do you have?
       다섯 권 있어요.   I have five.

   D. 남자친구 몇 명 있어요?   How many boyfriends do you have?
       여섯 명 있어요.   I have six.

   E. 여자친구 몇 명 있어요?   How many girlfriends do you have?
       네 명 있어요.   I have four.

   F. 개 몇 마리 있어요?   How many dogs do you have?
       없어요.   I don't have.

   G. 와인 몇 병 있어요?   How many bottles of wine do you have?
       한 병 있어요.   I have one.

5 A. 친구 있어요?   Do you have a friend?
       네. 있어요.   Yes. I have.
       친구 몇 명 있어요?   How many friends do you have?
       일곱 명 있어요.   I have 7 friends.

   B. 펜 있어요?   Do you have a pen?
       네. 있어요.   Yes. I have.
       펜 몇 개 있어요?   How many pens do you have?
       다섯 개 있어요.   I have 5.

C. 개 있어요? / Do you have a dog?
아니요. 없어요. / No. I don't have.
D. 책 있어요? / Do you have a book?
네. 있어요. / Yes. I have.
책 몇 권 있어요? / How many books do you have?
네 권 있어요. / I have 4.
E. 맥주 있어요? / Do you have beer?
아니요. 없어요. / No. I don't have.
F. 물 있어요? / Do you have water?
네. 있어요. / Yes. I have.
물 몇 병 있어요? / How many bottles of water do you have?
열한 병 있어요.3 / I have 11 bottles.

제 4 과 맥주 얼마예요?

1 A. 생일이 언제예요? / When is your birthday?
십이월 이십팔일 이에요. / It is December 28th.
몇 년생 이에요? / What year were you born in?
천구백팔십이 년생 이에요. / I was born in 1982.
몇 살 이에요? / How old are you?
서른 두 살 이에요. / I am 32 years old.
B. 생일이 언제예요? / When is your birthday?
일월 십오일 이에요. / It is January 15th.
몇 년생 이에요? / What year were you born in?
천구백칠십팔 년생 이에요. / I was born in 1978.
몇 살 이에요? / How old are you?
서른 여섯 살 이에요. / I am 36 years old.
C. 생일이 언제예요? / When is your birthday?
오월 팔일 이에요. / It is May 8th.
몇 년생 이에요? / What year were you born in?
천구백 팔십팔 년생 이에요. / I was born in 1988.
몇 살 이에요? / How old are you?
스물 여섯 살 이에요. / I am 26 years old.
D. 생일이 언제예요? / When is your birthday?
칠월 십구일 이에요. / It is July 19th.
몇 년생 이에요? / What year were you born in?
천구백칠십구 년생 이에요. / I was born in 1979.
몇 살 이에요? / How old are you?
서른다섯 살 이에요. / I am 35 years old.

Exercise Answer Key

이름 (name)	생일 (birthday)	출생 연도 (year of birth)	나이 (age)
A. 모건	12월 28일	1982	32
B. 상현	1월 15일	1978	36
C. 에이미	5월 8일	1988	26
D. 혜민	7월 19일	1979	35

2 A. 상현은 생일이 언제예요?   When is Sanghyun's birthday?

        일월 십오일 이에요.   It is January 15th.

    B. 에이미는 몇 년생 이에요?   What year was Amy born in?

        천 구백 팔십 팔 년생 이에요.   She was born in 1988.

    C. 혜민은 몇 살 이에요?   How old is Haemin?

        서른 다섯 살 이에요.   She is 35 years old.

3 A. 와인 얼마예요?   How much is the wine?

        팔천 오백원 이에요.   It is 8,500 won.

        와인 네 잔 주세요.   Please give me 4 glasses of wine.

        삼만 사천원 이에요.   It is 34,000 won.

    B. 공책 얼마예요?   How much is the notebook?

        천 오백원 이에요.   It is 1,5000 won.

        공책 두 권 주세요.   Please give me 2 notebooks.

        삼천원 이에요.   It is 3,000 won.

    C. 강아지 얼마예요?   How much is the puppy?

        오만원 이에요.   It is 50,000 won.

        강아지 두 마리 주세요.   Please give me 2 puppies.

        십만원 이에요.   It is 100,000 won.

    D. 스마트폰 얼마예요?   How much is the smartphone?

        오십 삼만 팔천원 이에요.   It is 538,000 won.

        스마트폰 세 개 주세요.   Please give me 3 smartphones.

        백 육십 일만 사천원 이에요.   It is 1,614,000 won.

4 A. 두 시 예요.   It is 2.

    B. 세시 사십 오분 이에요.   It is 3 45.

    C. 다섯 시 예요.   It is 5.

    D. 오전 한 시 예요.   It is 1 am.

    E. 오후 두시 삼십분 이에요.   It is 2 30 pm.

    F. 오전 열시 사십오분 이에요.   It is 10 45 am.

    G. 오후 열한시 이십오분 이에요.   It is 11 25 pm.

제 5 과 뭐 먹고 싶어요?

1 A. 뭐 먹고 싶어요?   What do you want to eat?
   해물파전 먹고 싶어요.   I want to eat green onion pancake with seafood.

   B. 뭐 마시고 싶어요?   What do you want to drink?
   녹차 마시고 싶어요.   I want to drink greentea.

   C. 뭐 보고 싶어요?   What do you want to watch(see)?
   뮤지컬 보고 싶어요.   I want to watch a musical.

   D. 뭐 공부하고 싶어요?   What do you want to study?
   수학 공부하고 싶어요.   I want to study mathematics.

   E. 어디 가고 싶어요?   Where do you want to go?
   제주도 가고 싶어요.   I want to go to Jeju island.

   F. 어디에서 자고 싶어요?   Where do you want to sleep?
   러브모텔에서 자고 싶어요.   I want to sleep in a love motel.

   G. 어디에서 살고 싶어요?   Where do you want to live?
   태국에서 살고 싶어요.   I want to live in Thailand.

2 A. 뭐 먹고 싶어요?   What do you want to eat?
   피자 하고 볶음밥 먹고 싶어요.   I want to eat pizza and fried rice.

   B. 뭐 마시고 싶어요?   What do you want to drink?
   소주 하고 커피 마시고 싶어요.   I want to drink soju and coffee.

   C. 뭐 보고 싶어요?   What do you want to watch(see)?
   영화 하고 뮤지컬 보고 싶어요.   I want to watch a movie and a musical.

   D. 뭐 공부하고 싶어요?   What do you want to study?
   한국어 하고 중국어 하고 토플 공부하고 싶어요.   I want to study Korean, Chinese and TOEFL.

   E. 어디 가고 싶어요?   Where do you want to go?
   러브모텔 하고 찜질방 하고 술집 가고 싶어요.   I want to go to a love motel, Korean style public bath and a bar.

   F. 어디에서 자고 싶어요?   Where do you want to sleep?
   호텔 하고 집에서 자고 싶어요.   I want to sleep at a hotel and at home.

   G. 어디에서 살고 싶어요?   Where do you want to live?
   태국하고 제주도에서 살고 싶어요.   I want to live in Thailand.

제 6 과 어디에서 데이트 해요?

1 A. 뭐 해요?   What do you do? (What are you doing?)
   공부 해요.   I study. (I am studying.)
   공부 잘 해요?   Do you study well? (Are you a good student?)
   아니요. 공부 잘 못 해요.   No. I don't study well. (I am not a good student.)

   B. 뭐 해요?   What do you do? (What are you doing?)
   노래 해요.   I sing. (I am singing.)
   노래 잘 해요?   Do you sing well? (Are you good at singing?)
   아니요. 노래 잘 못 해요.   No. I don't sing well. (I am not good.)

	C.	뭐 해요?	What do you do? (What are you doing?)
		일 해요.	I work. (I am working.)
		일 잘 해요?	Do you work well? (Are you a good worker?)
		네. 일 잘 해요.	Yes. I work well. (I am a good worker.)
	D.	뭐 해요?	What do you do? (What are you doing?)
		운동 해요.	I exercise. (I am exercising.)
		운동 잘 해요?	Do you exercise well? (Are you good at exercising?)
		네. 운동 잘 해요.	Yes. I exercise well. (I am good at exercising.)
	E.	뭐 해요?	What do you do? (What are you doing?)
		요리 해요.	I cook. (I am cooking.)
		요리 잘 해요?	Do you cook well? (Are you good at cooking?)
		네. 요리 잘 해요.	Yes. I cook well. (I am good at cooking.)
	F.	뭐 해요?	What do you do? (What are you doing?)
		운전 해요.	I drive. (I am driving.)
		운전 잘 해요?	Do you drive well? (Are you good at driving?)
		아니요. 운전 잘 못 해요.	No. I don't drive well. (I am not good at driving.)
2	A.	출근 전에 샤워 해요?	Do you take a shower before going to work?
		네. 샤워 해요.	Yes. I take a shower.
	B.	퇴근 후에 인터넷 해요?	Do you use the internet after you leave your office after work?
		아니요. 인터넷 안 해요.	No. I don't use the internet.
	C.	식사 전에 요리 해요?	Do you cook before the meal?
		네. 요리 해요.	Yes. I cook.
	D.	데이트 후에 샤워 해요?	Do you take a shower after a date?
		아니요. 샤워 안 해요.	No. I don't take shower.
3	A.	어디에서 데이트 해요?	Where do you go on a date?
		모텔에서 데이트 해요.	I date at a motel.
	B.	어디에서 쇼핑 해요?	Where do you go shopping?
		이마트에서 쇼핑 해요.	I go shopping to the E-Mart.
	C.	어디에서 샤워 해요?	Where do you take a shower?
		집에서 샤워 해요.	I take a shower at home.
	D.	어디에서 인터넷 해요?	Where do you use the internet.
		회사에서 인터넷 해요.	I use the internet at my company.
	E.	어디에서 일 해요?	Where do you work?
		찜질방에서 일 해요.	I work at a Korean style public bath.
	F.	어디에서 노래 해요?	Where do you sing?
		술집에서 노래 해요.	I sing at a bar.
4	A.	미국에 어떻게 가요?	How do you go to USA?
		비행기로 가요.	I go by an airplane.
	B.	제주도에 어떻게 가요?	How do you go to Jeju island?
		배로 가요.	I go by a boat.
	C.	이태원에 어떻게 가요?	How do you go to Itaewon?
		택시로 가요.	I go by a taxi.

D. 부산에 어떻게 가요?　　　　　How do you go to Busan?
　　기차로 가요.　　　　　　　　I go by a train.

제 7 과　우리, 같이 인도 음식 먹어요!

1 A.　뭐 봐요?　　　　　　　　　What do you watch?
　　　영화 봐요.　　　　　　　　I watch a movie.
　B.　뭐 먹어요?　　　　　　　　What do you eat?
　　　파스타 먹어요.　　　　　　I eat pasta.
　C.　뭐 마셔요?　　　　　　　　What do you drink?
　　　와인 마셔요.　　　　　　　I drink wine.
　D.　뭐 좋아해요?　　　　　　　What do you like?
　　　맥주 좋아해요.　　　　　　I like beer.
　E.　뭐 읽어요?　　　　　　　　What do you read?
　　　책 읽어요.　　　　　　　　I read a book.
　F.　뭐 만들어요?　　　　　　　What do you make?
　　　볶음밥 만들어요.　　　　　I make a fried rice.
　G.　뭐 사요?　　　　　　　　　What do you buy?
　　　스마트폰 사요.　　　　　　I buy a smartphone.
　H.　뭐 필요해요?　　　　　　　What do you need?
　　　인터넷 필요해요.　　　　　I need the internet.

2 A.　언제 선물을 줘요?　　　　　When do you give a gift?
　　　크리스마스에 선물을 줘요.　I give a gift on Christmas.
　B.　언제 애인을 만나요?　　　　When do you meet your lover?
　　　일곱시에 애인을 만나요.　　I meet the lover at 7.
　C.　언제 빵을 만들어요?　　　　When do you make bread?
　　　아침에 빵을 만들어요.　　　I make bread in the morning.
　D.　언제 책을 읽어요?　　　　　When do you read a book?
　　　밤에 책을 읽어요.　　　　　I read a book in the night.
　E.　언제 케익을 사요?　　　　　When do you buy a cake?
　　　생일에 케익을 사요.　　　　I buy a cake on a birthday.
　F.　언제 한국어를 배워요?　　　When do you learn Korean?
　　　다섯시 이십 오분에 한국어를 배워요.　I learn Korean at 5:25.

3 A.　클럽 좋아해요?　　　　　　Do you like a club?
　　　네. 클럽 좋아해요.　　　　Yes. I like a club.
　　　우리, 같이 클럽 가요.　　　Let's go to a club together.
　　　좋아요. 같이 클럽 가요.　　Let's go to a club together.

Exercise Answer Key

B. 뮤지컬 좋아해요?
Do you like a musical?

네. 뮤지컬 좋아해요.
Yes. I like a musical.

우리, 같이 뮤지컬 봐요.
Let's watch a musical together.

좋아요. 같이 뮤지컬 봐요.
Good. Let's watch a musical together.

C. 커피 좋아해요?
Do you like coffee?

네. 커피 좋아해요.
Yes. I like coffee.

우리, 같이 커피 마셔요.
Let's drink coffee together.

좋아요. 같이 커피 마셔요.
Good. Let's drink coffee together.

D. 요가 좋아해요?
Do you like yoga?

네. 요가 좋아해요.
Yes. I like yoga.

우리, 같이 요가 배워요.
Let's learn yoga together.

좋아요. 같이 요가 배워요.
Good. Let's learn yoga together.

E. 소녀시대 좋아해요?
Do you like Girl's Generation?

네. 소녀시대 좋아해요.
Yes. I like Girl's Generation.

우리, 같이 소녀시대 만나요.
Let's meet Girl's Generation together.

좋아요. 같이 소녀시대 만나요
Good. Let's meet Girl's Generation together.

4 A. 우리, 같이 부산 가요.
Let's go to Busan together.

부산은 그냥 그래요.
Busan is just okay.

제주도는 어때요?
How about Jeju island?

좋아요. 같이 제주도 가요.
Good. Let's go to Jeju island together.

B. 우리, 같이 영화 봐요.
Let's watch a movie together.

영화는 그냥 그래요.
Movie is just okay.

뮤지컬은 어때요?
How about a musical?

좋아요. 같이 뮤지컬 봐요.
Good. Let's watch a musical together.

C. 우리, 같이 커피 마셔요.
Let's drink coffee together.

커피는 그냥 그래요.
Coffee is just okay.

와인은 어때요?
How about wine?

좋아요. 같이 와인 마셔요.
Good. Let's drink wine together.

D. 우리, 같이 중국어 배워요.
Let's learn Chinese together.

중국어는 그냥 그래요.
Chinese is just okay.

스페인어는 어때요?
How about Spanish?

좋아요. 같이 스페인어 배워요.
Good. Let's learn Spanish together.

E. 우리, 같이 싸이 만나요.
Let's meet Psy together.

싸이는 그냥 그래요.
Psy is just okay.

소녀시대는 어때요?
How about Girl's Generation?

좋아요. 같이 소녀시대 만나요.
Good. Let's meet Girl's Generation together.

제 8 과   머리하고 목이 아파요.

1 A. 이거 뭐예요?   What is this?
    손가락이에요.   It is a finger.
    손가락 몇 개 있어요?   How many fingers do you have?
    열 개 있어요.   I have 10.

  B. 이거 뭐예요?   What is this?
    다리예요.   This is a leg.
    다리 몇 개 있어요?   How many legs do you have?
    두 개 있어요.   I have 2.

  C. 이거 뭐예요?   What is this?
    머리카락이에요.   It is hair.
    머리카락 몇 개 있어요?   How many hairs do you have?
    많이 있어요.   I have many.

2 A. 어디가 아파요?   Where does it hurt?
    배 아파요.   My stomach hurts.
    어떤 병원에 가요?   What kind of clinic do you go?
    내과에 가요.   I go to an internal medicine clinic.

  B. 어디가 아파요?   Where does it hurt?
    이 아파요.   My teeth hurt.
    어떤 병원에 가요?   What kind of clinic do you go?
    치과에 가요.   I go to a dental clinic.

  C. 어디가 아파요?   Where does it hurt?
    눈 아파요.   My eyes hurt.
    어떤 병원에 가요?   What kind of clinic do you go?
    안과에 가요.   I go to an ophthalmology.

3 A. 어디가 아파요?   Where does it hurt?
    목하고 배가 아파요.   My throat and stomach hurt.

  B. 어디가 아파요?   Where does it hurt?
    팔하고 다리가 아파요.   My arms and legs hurt.

4 A. 어디가 아파요?   Where does it hurt?
    머리가 아프고 열 나요.   My head hurts and I have fever.

  B. 어디가 아파요?   Where does it hurt?
    목이 아프고 기침 해요.   My throat hurts and I cough.

제 9 과   내일 뭐 할 거예요?

1 A. 내일 뭐 할 거예요?   What will you do tomorrow?
    도서관 갈 거예요.   I will go to the library.

Exercise Answer Key

B. 크리스마스에 뭐 할 거예요? — What will you do on Christmas?
친구 만날 거예요. — I will meet a friend.

C. 설날에 뭐 할 거예요? — What will you do on Lunar new year?
한국어 공부할 거예요. — I will study Korean.

D. 주말에 뭐 할 거예요? — What will you do this weekend?
영화 볼 거예요. — I will watch a movie.

E. 석가탄신일에 뭐 할 거예요? — What will you do on Buddha's birthday?
개고기 먹을 거예요. — I will eat dog meat.

F. 생일에 뭐 할 거예요? — What will you do on your birthday?
와인 마실 거예요. — I will drink wine.

2 A. 크리스마스에 뭐 할 거예요? — What will you do on Christmas?
제주도 갈 거예요. — I will go to Jeju island.
누구랑 갈 거예요? — With whom will you go?
친구랑 갈 거예요. — I will go with a friend.
어떤 친구랑 갈 거예요? — What kind of friend will you go with?
남자친구랑 갈 거예요. — I will go with my boyfriend.
남자친구 누구예요? — Who is your boyfriend?
몰라도 돼요. — You don't need to know.

B. 생일에 뭐 할 거예요? — What will you do on your birthday?
영화 볼 거예요. — I will watch a movie.
어디에서 볼 거예요? — Where will you watch?
명동에서 볼 거예요. — I will watch in Myeongdong.
누구랑 볼 거예요? — With whom will you watch?
신경 끄세요. — Mind your own business.

제 10 과   토요일에 뭐 했어요?

1 A. 화요일에 뭐 했어요? — What did you do on Tuesday?
친구랑 놀았어요. — I hung out with a friend.

B. 목요일에 뭐 했어요? — What did you do on Thursday?
영어 공부했어요. — I studied English.

C. 지난 주말에 뭐 했어요? — What did you do last weekend?
소설 읽었어요. — I read a novel.

D. 지난주 금요일에 뭐 했어요? — What did you do last Friday?
여자친구랑 싸웠어요. — I fought with my girlfriend.

2 A. 목요일에 뭐 했어요? — What did you do on Tuesday?
집에서 놀고 도서관에서 한국어 공부했어요. — I hung out at home and studied Korean at a library.

B. 지난 주말에 뭐 했어요? — What did you do last weekend?
여자친구랑 싸우고 강아지랑 놀았어요. — I fought with my girlfriend and played with my puppy.

C. 지난주 금요일에 뭐 했어요? — What did you do on Tuesday?
집에서 신문 읽고 모텔에서 잤어요. — I read newspaper at home and slept at a motel.

Did you enjoy this book?

Do you want to learn more?

Are you ready to speak Wild Korean?

We have the next step for you.

A Fieldguide to Real Korean Conversation
For Beginner to Intermediate Levels

야생 한국어
Wild Korean 2nd Edition
Sanghyun Ahn

Made in the USA
Columbia, SC
18 September 2019